THE NINE GLENS

A personal look at the

history, folklore and poetry

of the

Nine Glens of Antrim.

by

MAUREEN DONNELLY

A

First Published — December, 1974

Reprinted — June, 1975

Revised Edition — April, 1977

Reprinted — June, 1983

Revised November 1987

Reprinted March 1991

Cover Picture: LURIGETHAN IN SPRING

By: ALAN JOHNSTON

ISBN 0 948154 40 3

I wish to thank all the people who encouraged me to write this very personal account of the Nine Glens especially the McFetridge families of Cushendun and Cushendall, the Donnelly family of Ballycastle and my many friends in the Glens.

I am most grateful to the poets Sydney Bell, the late John Hewitt and the late Harry Browne for allowing me to use their work. Thanks are also due to Miss Susan Shrine for permission to use the poems of Moira O'Neill; the late D. J. Murphy to print the poems of Siobhan Ni Luain; the trustees of Florence Wilson for the use of her poem; and Messrs. Gill and Macmillan for permission to quote extracts from "The Black North".

I am indebted to Hugh Alexander Boyd, the well-known historian for reading my script and lending me some rare historical material; to my sister-in-law Brenda McFetridge and my son Mark for the illustrations; and my patient husband for his invaluable help in so many ways.

In this edition I am delighted to have the photographs of Alan Johnston and would also like to thank the Tourist Board for permission to use their photograph on page 112.

M.D.

Photographs in this edition are by ALAN JOHNSTON (except pages 26, 79 and 112).

4

TO MY FATHER AND MOTHER

THE NINE GLENS

There are nine Glens of Antrim
That run down to the sea,
There are nine Glens of Antrim
And all are dear to me,
Glenarm, Glencorp, Glenaan, Glencloy,
Glenariff and Glendun,
Glen-bally-eamon and Glentow,
And Glenshesk of the Sun.

On Torr Head Road.

In this book I wish to share my pleasure in the people, the places, the traditions of song, story and verse, with others who also feel that the beauty of scenery is but a small part of the total "treasure" of the Glens.

MAUREEN DONNELLY

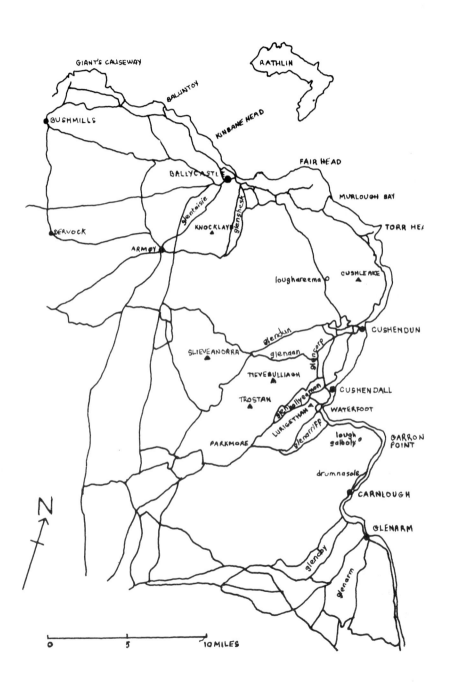

Contents

PART I — FROM GLEN TO GLEN

PART II — THE PEOPLE OF THE GLENS

PART III — BELIEFS AND CUSTOMS

PART I

FROM GLEN TO GLEN

THE GLENS AND THE MEANINGS OF THEIR NAMES

GLENARM	Glen of the armed force
GLENCLOY	Glen of the dykes (or sword)
GLENARIFF	Glen of the plough, or arable glen
GLENBALLYEAMON	Glen of Edward's town
GLENAAN or GLENGORM	Hemmed-in or Blue Glen, or Glen of the Proverb or little glen
GLENCORP or GLENCORB	Glen of the corpses or of the coaches
GLENDUN	Glen of the Dun (brown) river
GLENSHESK	Glen of the sedges
GLENTAISIE or GLENTOW	Glen of Taise (daughter of a King of Rathlin)

Where the Glen is known by different names I have placed the most popular first. Scholars differ as to the meanings but I decided here to set down all the choices for the interest of the reader.

Glencloy (glean-cloidhe, the bank or brow) is full of dykes (stone walls or ditches); so it is my choice. But some think the glen is shaped like a sword: broad near the sea, then narrowing to a point, hence the "sword" meaning..

Glenaan is called **Glengorm** (blue glen) in an old poem by Joseph Campbell. In other places it is referred to as the "Glen of the little ford" or the "Glen of the Proverb." It could be "Little glen" according to Joyce.

B

Glencorp is **Glencorb** in the Shell Guide to Ireland. It is "Glenkearin," according to Professor W. Clarke Robinson. This is very possible as St. Kieran was the Patron Saint of the Old Layde Church, but I have never seen this name used anywhere else. Also the surname McIlheran (son of the disciple of Kieran) is found in the district.

There is a **Glenkearn** near Ballycastle not usually counted as one of the nine glens. "Caorain" in Irish means bog-land and I wonder if some confusion between that and "Kieran" ever occurred.

"Glen of the coaches" is a rare meaning of Glencorp.

Glentaisie is the more popular name for the little glen near Knocklayd, but Glentow is also used. It is the Glen of Taise. Taise was a daughter of a King of Rathlin and was sought as a wife by the King of Norway. He invaded Rathlin and after many battles was killed. **"It is better** than the enjoyment of a feast how we have fought the great **battle,"** said Taise when it was all over!

Cushendun.

COAST ROAD

The man that made the roadway
  From Larne to Cushendall,
The people say that in a way
  'Twas little he did at all;
He broke the rock and boulder,
  He drove the pathway through
But — A fairy sat on his shoulder
  And showed him the thing to do.

The glory of Glenariffe,
  The crags of Garron Head,
The shingled beach, the sandy reach,
  The whins in glory spread;
The man that made the roadway,
  O fine the plans he drew,
But — A fairy sat on his shoulder
  And showed him the thing to do.

The distant misty headland,
  The glen and winding way,
The loom of the Mull, the wheeling gull,
  The lash of the angry spray;
The man that planned the roadway,
  He kept these things in view,
But — A fairy sat on his shoulder
  And showed him the thing to do.

Here where MacDonnell clansmen
  Battled to hold Glenarm,
The storied past is prisoned fast
  In castle and cot and farm;
The man that made the roadway
  His ancient history knew,
But — A fairy sat on his shoulder
  And showed him the thing to do.

And he who makes the journey
  Along the road today,
To left and right, for his delight,
  Are river and cliff and bay;
The man that made the roadway,
  He planned it well and true,
But — A fairy sat on his shoulder
  And showed him the thing to do.

H. Browne.

FROM GLEN TO GLEN

The **Coast Road** is the beckoning ribbon that leads me to the Glens and when I pass through the **Black Arch,** just outside Larne, I have stepped through the magic casement to my "special" country.

On one side the lusty breakers, foam-tipped, crash against the man-made barriers which support the road, and on the other the green undulating glens spill out their grand beauties towards the coast. Gouged by ancient glaciers the famous Nine Glens, each with its own special character, spread their charms for our delight.

For almost 100 miles the **Antrim Coast Road** winds its way round stern headlands and delightful bays. Green slopes of hillside dip gently towards the road, and massive cliffs of delightful contrasting colour, black basalt, white limestone, red sandstone tower threateningly above the road. As a small child I found it hard to conceal my terror as the 'bus in which I travelled passed under these great overhangs. Many of them have gone now with improvements made after recent dangerous subsidences.

Yet the grim cliffs were but one of the many landmarks for this journey that I loved. Just beside the **Black Arch** is a beautiful bay called, in English, **Drains Bay.** This name conjures up an unsavoury picture, but the original name in Irish was **Cuan an Dhroighneain — Bay of the Blackthorns.** A pity it was ever changed!

Here, too, about five miles out to sea are **The Maidens** — two lighthouse rocks side by side with their twinkling lights: a special delight to spot in the dark night sea.

On a rock beneath the promontory of **Ballygalley** stand the ruins of an old Castle called **Carn Castle.** It was supposed to have been erected by a prince of old to protect his daughter from the attentions of an unworthy suitor! But a less romantic explanation seems more likely: that the castle was built by one Duncan Fitzgilbert, a Welsh adventurer, to whom King John had granted lands in the Larne - Glenarm area.

BALLYGALLEY

Next we see another old castle, now a modern hotel. It has been called **O'Halloran's Castle**, but by right it should be **Shaw's Castle**, having been built by James Shaw in 1625 and occupied by his family for over 200 years. This old fortress has seven-foot thick walls and has withstood many assaults in its 350 years of history.

But the most celebrated story associated with Ballygalley is the rather bizarre tale of Jean Park, who used to live in a little hut on the beach. This is her story.

"A boat once drifted into Ballygalley Bay. In it were a dead woman and a little baby, alive, but scarcely a day old. Where they had come from no one knew. A coastguard took the baby home and called her Marina Jane. She grew up to be a beautiful girl and married a sailor called Park, who also owned a farm. For many years after the marriage her husband was both sailor and farmer and they were content.

When absent on one of his voyages Jane had a dream that he would never return. Daily she used to go down to the beach to look for signs of a boat bringing him back to her. This went on for a long time, the farm was neglected and the husband never returned. Kindly neighbours did what they could for the poor woman, but the inevitable happened; bailiffs arrived one day and Jane was thrown out of her cottage which was boarded up.

With her own hands she then built a hut on the beach, and gathered limpets for food. Her faithful dog, Brinie, seldom left her side. Brinie even had four puppies in the little hut on the beach.

One night a terrible storm blew up and the sea rose threatingly. A neighbour tried to persuade Jane to come to his house for shelter, but she would not leave in case her husband might turn up.

The dog Brinie tried to pull her out by the dress, but Jane would not budge. Brinie did, however, manage to carry her wee pups to safety, one by one.

Next morning there was no sign of the hut nor of Jane. She came from the sea, and to the sea she had returned."

GLENARM

Of all the glens on Antrim Coast
  Glenarm's the glen to see:
Green hills and woods it has to boast,
  Blue bay and shining quay,
Bright birds and flowers in sunny bowers,
  Sweet river flowing free;
Strange legends old, so long untold;
  Fair scenes of festive glee;

The spire, where ancient ivy climbs,
  The church mid bowering trees,
The tower that peals the evening chimes,
  The flag that flouts the breeze;
The chapel, courthouse, fountain, mill,
  The school by castle bridge,
The houses clustering up the hill,
  The plantin' on the ridge.

Here Scotia's earliest settlers stood
  On Erin's emerald strand—
The Bissets, blamed for Athol's blood,
  With feigned crusading band
Made Antrim's glens their Palestine,
  And spread along the shore,
Till Margery, last of Bisset's line,
  Espoused MacDonnell More,

From whom the Earls of Antrim sprung,
  Who reared the castle grey,
Where doughty deeds were seen or sung
  That echo till our day;
Round ivy towers, in parks and bowers,
  Flit doves and pheasants gay;
The hare and deer sport safely here,
  The trout and salmon play.

W. Clarke Robinson

On the way to Glenarm we come to the "White" area where the white chalk cliffs make a vivid contrast to the bright green of the grass and the deep blue of the sea. It is a subsidence area and has given trouble to the road builders. On the steep hillsides ridges are a special feature. Here potatoes were once cultivated in terraces, but now the sheep have taken over.

THE FLOWERS

The beauty of the wild flowers that run riot in the secret places of the glens is a joy to the heart. As I child I never knew their botanical names but their sweet perfections, welcoming each new season, were well known to me. The slopes along the coast especially are star-studded with primroses in the springtime; and in the damp places at the bottom wave the lovely yellow Irises. Wild Hyacinths and early Purple Orchis also abound.

According to Praegar some plants were found in this area which are really characteristic of North Britain — the Wood Crane's Bill, the Wood Cow-Wheat, the Tea-Leaved Willow and Few-Flowered Sedge.

On the plateau near Garron grew two sedges — Carex pauciflora and Carex magellanica, unknown elsewhere in Ireland. There can also be found the rare Yellow Marsh Saxifrage.

It was sufficient for us as children to know that after the primroses came the cascades of "bucky" roses, white, pink and red, and those giant Fairy Thimbles. The wee yellow flowers that sprinkled the moorland we loved, and the fuchsia hedges waved above us, reminding us of fairy lanterns. Then came the purple heather and the gold of bracken and bright berry-laden rowans and haws and blaze of holly set in rich dark green. I will never forget the smell of honeysuckle, pervading my summer childhood of the warm wet days.

It and the long buttercups were the warm-clutched flowers for the jam-jar in the wee square window of the back kitchen, the homely, turf-scented, clock-ticking place, where the crickets lived.

Glenarm.

GLENARM

At **Glenarm,** a neat seaside town with its castle and churches, is the first glen.

This is a privately-owned glen on the estate of the Earl of Antrim, the chief dwelling-place of the Macdonnells since 1636. The inscription over the entrance to the Castle reads:

WITH THE LEAVE OF
GOD, THIS CASTLE
WAS BUILT BY SIR
RANDLE McDONNEL
KNIGHT, ERLE OF ANTRIM,
HAVEING TO HIS
WIFE, DAME AELLIS
O'NILL, IN THE YEAR
OF OUR LORD GOD, 1636.

This stone with inscription is now incorporated in the Barbican entrance in Castle Street.

The glen is well wooded, with a brown, stony river spanned by attractive old bridges. There is a deer park here too. Richard Dobbs in his **"Description of the County of Antrim 1683"** writes:

"Yet above the town is the glen through which the river runs, and is clad with underwoods, is the pleasantest hunting for buck that ever I saw, and you may ride in either side, and have the dogs or bucks, or both continually in view, and stand in a manner still for two hours together."

I find this deerpark of special interest, not just because I enjoyed a camp there as a Girl Guide, but because it was here my grandfather lived as a boy before he and his brothers settled in the Cushendall area. Their name, "McFetridge," a sub clan of the O'Bresslans of Donegal, has for long been associated with the MacDonnells. In an old account of a battle at Dunluce Castle in 1641, a certain Captain McPhedris is reported to have been given warning that this MacDonnell stronghold was about to be attacked by the O'Neills. McPhedris means, "son of Peter," and many of the name, though the spelling is different nowadays, continue to live in the Glen.

Near the Castle can be traced the remains of the old church of Templeoughter, the upper church.

In the townland of **Solar** nearby was another ancient church, the Bell of which, made of thin sheet iron, is in the Ulster Museum.

Shane O'Neill's[*]body, according to one legend, is supposed to have been brought to Glenarm for burial after his murder at Cushendun.

A local story relates:

"**A holy friar came from Armagh to the Abbot of Glenarm, and said, "Father, I come from our brothers of Armagh to beg of you that you will permit us to remove the body of the great O'Neill for the purpose of interment in the tomb of his ancestors in Armagh."**

The Abbot of Glenarm paused for a moment before replying, "Have you," said he, "brought with you the remains of James Macdonnell,[*] Lord cf Antrim and Cantire, who was buried among the strangers of Armagh?" The friar answered that he had not brought the wished-for remains. "Then," replied the Abbot, "whilst you continue to tread on the grave of James, Lord of Antrim and Cantire, know ye, that we, here in Glenarm, will continue to trample on the dust of the great O'Neill."

On the seaward side of the Coast Road, just beyond Glenarm, is a heap of rocks with an opening, called "the madman's window" where someone is supposed to have committed suicide. This was another of my "shivery" places. Not far away on a slope is Straidkilly, the slipping village. Inch by inch this eerie, deserted village moves slowly towards the sea.

GLENCLOY

This garden-like glen steps out to the sea at Carnlough. It is a favourite spot for photographers and painters. Its white chalk quarries, bursting through the hillside, make a vivid splash of brightness among the little patchwork fields which surround them. The fields are neatly bounded by lacey, stone "dykes" which gives the Glen its name. Glencloy has also been known as Glencule.

Note: Shane O'Neill (see page 38).

Note: James MacDonnell had been starved to death in O'Neill's dungeon!

C

By Drumnasole on the Coast Road.

CARNLOUGH

At the foot of Glencloy, **Carnlough** is a gay seaside place, with a busy little harbour where steamers used to export chalk to Scotland.

Just behind the town are the Cranny Falls situated in a deep little well-wooded glen. A visit here is a pleasant afternoon's walk along a quiet river-bank.

The Doonan (Little fort) Falls are also close by Carnlough, on the east side of the Doonan river, a tributary of the Glencloy River.

The Drumnasole Waterfalls, farther to the north, are approached by a passage named the "Goat's Parlour." At the bottom of this path is Tubberdoney, a well believed to help cure afflictions of the eye.

On the great headland of **Drumnasole** the Antrim Scots communicated by beacon fires with their kinsmen across the Sea of Moyle (the North Channel). Drumnasole means "the ridge of light." The Dungallon Fort nearby is said to be the last fort in Ireland to be held by the Danes.

These early journeys I made round this intriguing coast were always by 'bus for it was wartime and petrol was scarce and communications difficult. Leaving the bombs and terror of Belfast and entering this world of beauty and peace with its kindly inhabitants has made the Glens for ever a "haven" in my mind.

It was so pleasant to proceed at a leisurely pace into the Glens country, lifting bags of letters at tiny post-offices like Garron, helping the country folk on and off with their parcels and baskets of cheeping chicks, while all the while the soft Glens' accent, akin to Highland-Scots, lapped around me, adding to my close-hugged pleasure. I eavesdropped unashamedly on the local "crack," and knew I belonged.

Above Garron Point,* the great promontory of **Dunmaul** (the bald fort) dominates the landscape. Away up on the cliff behind Garron, but hidden from the road, is **Garron Tower**. It was built partly as relief work after the famine of 1848-1849 and was the home of the Londonderry family. It is now a co-educational grammar school.

SAINT MacNISSI AND GARRON

Near Ardclinis Bridge* farther round on the coast road is the old Ardclinis Church. Until about 1760 an ancient crozier or pastoral staff rested on the ruined chancel window. This is thought to have belonged to St. Oengus MacNisse or MacNissi, who is regarded as the founder of the monastic See of Connor, in A.D. 506. It is said that once the crozier was used for administering oaths.

Known as the Ardclinis Crozier, it was originally about 3ft. 2 ins. long, with a staff of Irish oak, protected by a covering of bronze terminating in a crook. The bronze head was overlaid with thin plates of silver. There was a crude representation of the Crucifixon rivetted to the staff, and the outline of a sheep's head among trefoils was another of its ornamentations.

St. Oengus MacNissi is believed to have founded the Christian Church of Ardclinis and to have been buried there. The boys' college at Garron Tower bears the name of the Saint.

Note: "Garron (a shrubbery) or Gearr-rin (short point).
Note: "Ardclinis — Ard-claoin-inse, the height of the sloping island.

O'Laverty, who had seen the Crozier, relates that about 1860 it was discovered that the crozier was in the possession of a farmer living on the mountain above Glenarm. He used it to dip into water, which he then administered to sick cows! When seen, it was being used as a peg to hold up yarn. It had been in the farmer's family for several generations.

The present home of the Ardclinis Crozier is the National Museum in Dublin. I am indebted to the Rev. Father Kevin Donnelly, once curate of Glenarm, for the following details:

"A certain bishop, who had to flee, left the crozier in the care of the Galvin family of Glendun with instructions to keep it in case he did not return. As he did not return the crozier was handed down as a family heirloom.

This Galvin family came to reside at Croc-an-dhu near Glenarm. One of the Galvin family married into the Magill Mor family. One of the Magills, Mrs. Eily McAllister, Aghaboy, had custody of the crozier, and in 1964 she decided to sell it to the National Museum. Contact was made through Mr. John O'Loan and Mr. David Kennedy, who then negotiated the sale. The money raised was donated towards the renovation of Feystown Church, Glenarm, where a replica of the crozier is to be seen on the Altar Rails door.

The crozier had been used for all kinds of purposes and from being stirred in pots, etc., the whole shaft had been burnt away. Some of the stones too were missing. It has now been carefully cleaned and restored."

AT SEA

'Tis the long blue Head of Garron
    From the sea,
Och, we're sailin' past the Garron
    On the sea.
Now Glen Ariff lies behind,
Where the waters fall and wind
By the willows o' Glen Ariff to the sea.

Ould Luirgedan rises green
    By the sea,
Ay, he stands between the Glens
    An' the sea.
Now we're past the darklin' caves,
Where the breaking summer waves
Wandher in wi' their trouble from the sea.

Moira O'Neill

We pass now the "Dog's nose" about three miles beyond Garron, so called because of its shape or because of the "coldness" of the spot and we come to a well-loved landmark.

Just past the old inn at Cloghastucan, where trace horses were kept for the Foaran Path, an old route to **Red Bay** over the mountains, is the **"White Lady"** (Clough na Stookan)* She is a white limestone pillar worn to the shape of a "lady." Her hair is piled high, and she wears a long dress with a delightful bustle. Incidentally this stone was once thought to be the most northerly point in Ireland.

A little farther along is another stone, the "white lady's grandmother," which is not so well known. Here is a grey stooped, shawled figure with a mossy bundle of sticks on her back, bending towards the mountain. I always felt sorry for granny, comparing her industry to "madame show-off" in the bustle!

THE CUSHENDALL COACH

The fields and farms are white with snow.
The moon is on the wane;
The coach that ran to Cushendall
Is out on the road again;
The ghostly wheels go rumbling round,
But they leave no mark or stain.

The coach that ran to Cushendall
Goes crunching through the snow;
The steaming horses step again
The roads they used to know,
And spectral drivers crack the whips
They cracked so long ago.

Note: "Clough na Stookan, stone of the pinnacle or stump.

White-faced passengers sit within,
In rug and tippet and shawl;
They lean across to the rattling door
To watch the snowflakes fall;
"O drear and long," they seem to say,
"The road to Cushendall."

Along, along by Drumnasole,
Along by Fallowvee,
On one hand looms the gloomy hills;
On the other the lonely sea.
As the ghostly coach-horn wakes again
The echoes that used to be.

And he who hears that echoing horn
Like a ghostly View Hallo
Will stare as the phantom coach goes by
On the road that it used to go—
A phantom coach with rattling wheels
That leave no mark in the snow.

H. Browne

Lurigethan, the great flat-topped mountain with its patchwork spreading skirts flowing over Cushendall, was one of the first mountains I could recognise and name. On one side is the glorious deep Glenariff spilling to the sea at the little village of **Waterfoot,** and on the other, the narrower, less populous **Glen Ballyeamon.**

GLENARIFF

With its scattering of white farmhouses and tiny farms, **Glenariff** is the largest and probably the most famous glen, spoiled a little for me by the man-made "tourist" walks in the middle. This glen has glorious waterfalls, **Ess-na-larach**—sometimes called "the tears of the mountain"—being one of the loveliest. Ess-na-larach means "the mare's fall," and **Ess-na-Crub** "the fall of the hoof." Along the flat bottom of the glen the Glenariff river winds leisurely seaward. Across the mouth of the Glen is the friendly little village of Waterfoot where the Glens Feis*is held. Waterfoot is sometimes called Glenariff.

Note: "Feis — a festival of song and music (see page 98).

Glenariff from Waterfoot.

I always like to make my homeward journey from the Glens by way of Ballymena and Glenariff, for the waterfalls and the soft greenness of trees and fields seem to fit my sad leave-taking mood more than the exhilarating splendours of the coastal journey.

On Lurig there is a cave called **Lig-na-Fenia,** surrounded by a ditch. This is "the hollow of the giants" who are said to have once lived there. **Finn MacCool*** was the leader of the "giants" and **Ossian,** whose grave is in Glenaan, was his warrior poet son. There is an old Danish fort, **Dun-Clana-Mourna** on the top of Lurig.

Tivera, a dear little rounded hill, a "fairy hill" according to the locals, a volcanic plug according to the geographers, can be seen now across Red Bay. It is a homely place at this distance but a "gentle" (supernatural) place when you are really there. Tivera means Hill of the Fort.

Note: Finn MacCool (see page 95).

RED BAY

We are now in the "Red" area where the sandstone on the landward side is pitted with caves, used as dwellings all down the years until recent times. There is a cave here known as Nanny's Cave, which in the 1800s was inhabited by a self-sufficient old woman called Ann Murray. She supported herself by knitting and spinning and the profits from selling a "drop of the native" (poteen). She was jailed for the last activity, but her penalty was wisely mitigated. Later she got round her difficulty by selling "glasses of water" and giving away a drop of whiskey with it! She died on 23rd March, 1847, aged 100.

Another cave here was used as a smith's forge, and still others were at times used by smugglers for their stores. In 1849 workmen found two bronze axes, a stone axe, and some silver coins in what was once a cave.

Red Bay Castle, above the Red Arch, is the ruin of a 16th century castle built by Sir James MacDonnell. It stands on an artificial hill thrown up as a fortress in the 12th or 13th century. Shane O'Neill destroyed it once. It was rebuilt by Sorley Boy in 1568, but then finally destroyed by the Cromwellian Garrison of Carrickfergus about 1652.

GLENBALLYEAMON

On the other side of Lurig from Glenariff this wide, deep glen sweeps down towards the little town of **Cushendall,** the very heart of the Glens. Occasionally one can glimpse the outlines of ancient forts, but now it is a fairly bare glen echoing only to the lonely bleating of the many sheep on its hillside. At the top of this Glen is the terminus of the old narrow-gauge railway and the ruins of "Retreat Castle." There is supposed to be a fairy tunnel here, too, where fairy music is said to try to lure the unwary. Beware!

To the right, looking up the Glen, is **Tievebulliagh,** the pointed hill beloved of painters and famous as a flint factory of early man. Flints were exported from here to other parts of the British Isles, and even as far afield as Europe.

Ahead you can see the great rounded cone of **Trostan,** at 1,817 feet the highest mountain in County Antrim.

BALLYEAMON CRADLE SONG

Rest tired eyes awhile,
Sweet is thy baby smile;
Angels are guarding and watch o'er thee;
Sleep, Ian grah mo chree,
Here on your mother's knee,
Angels are guarding and watch o'er thee.

Chorus :

The birdeens sing a fluting song;
They sing for thee the whole day long;
Wee fairies dance in dell and glade
For very love of thee,
The primrose in the sheltered nook,
The crystal stream, the babbling brook;
God gave you these His hands had made
For very love of thee.

Dream Ian grah mo chree,
Here on your mother's knee,
Angels are guarding and watch o'er thee;
Twilight and shadows fall,
Peace to the childher small;
Angels are guarding and watch o'er thee.

Keevers Douglas

CUSHENDALL

When I got as far as the dear, cosy town of Cushendall I felt I was "there." It surely deserves the title of the "heart of the Glens — ''the town.''

Cushendall from MacDonnell's Castle, Red Bay.

Here you find the pulse of the neighbourhood, the news, the gossip, the goings-on of the Glens.

Many of my relations had businesses here. They seemed to have a go at everything. They were builders, milk-roundsmen, garage owners, shop owners, etc. One of my

D

father's uncles had a saddler's business. Later, after it
closed, part of it was taken to the Museum in Belfast. That
same man used to run "charabancs," big, open, long cars
with folded-down roofs, which had to be hastily erected
when the rain came on. One of the many varied jobs my
father did was to drive tourists in these; a friendly
guide he must have been. Once, after a visit to the Lammas Fair in Ballycastle, he had to get help to carry his
"fares" back to the car—some had had a little too much!

You go over the bridge spanning the shallow brown Dall
river, where the fat trout meander, and you are right in the
middle of the town at the crossroads beside the square
curfew tower. Here the "boys" like to gather for a crack,
but at one time this tower was a jail and here, too, a curfew
bell was rung every night. Behind the tower is a steep,
steep hill leading to the "old" or "middle" road to
Cushendun. One passes the old fair green where fairs were
held not so long ago.

Turn left at the tower to follow the road to Cushendun.
On the right the very steep hill descending to the main
street is Martin's Court, where a "court" or fine house was
once built. I remember it chiefly as a marvellous place for
rolling whin-dyed Easter eggs. The wee school house on
the top welcomed me with a party every Christmas, cosy
with oil-lamps, a big blazing fire and "hunt the thimble" — and buns!

"Dusty Rhodes," (real name **James Stoddard Moore**),
who was born at Glenaan, near Cushendall, in 1884, ex-
presses his love for the place in this poem:

BUNANDALLA (Cushendall)

I've seen the Ghauts of Hindostan,
  Canton's pagodas gay,
I've seen the Burmese valleys,
  Where the ounce and leopard stray,
And all the fairest scenes on earth.
  I've viewed them o'er and o'er,
Yet I sigh for Bunandalla,
  On Antrim's rocky shore.

But oft I think on bygone times,
  When I used to ramble there;
But now alas! I find myself
  Bow'd down by age and care,
I cast my longing eyes around.
  I look for peace in vain;
Then I sigh for Bunandalla
  And its pleasant scenes again.

I used to climb Luirgedan's slopes,
  And Trostan's lofty brow,
And gaze on scenes of beauty
  That I cannot gaze on now,
For now I miss the sunny hills,
  I miss the mour.tain gale,
And I sigh for Bunandalla
  In the land of Innisfail.

On Crock-na-creigh I've oftimes sat
  In the long bright summer's day;
Embowered in woods beneath my feet
  The peaceful village lay.
Ah! beauteous spot; in earth's wide realms
  A fairer scene there's none.
So I sigh for Bunandalla
  And its ivied ruins lone.

By the flowery hill of Tieve-a-raw,
  Where elfin watchfires glow,
By the wooded slopes of sweet Shramore,
  Where Dalla's waters flow.
By Alt-a-cooin's sylvan shades
  'Twas there I used to stray,
Ere I left thee Bunandalla
  And they flowery valleys gay.

Alas! I cannot now return
  To scenes I loved so well,
To Knockanbuadh's fairy knoll,
  Or Conliem's woody dell.
Yet oft I'll think of Garron Point,
  Or Nappin's woodlands fair,
And sigh for Bunandalla
  And the scenes of beauty there.

The name "**Cushendall**" intrigues people. It should be pronounced "cush" as in "hush," not c'oo'sh. It is taken to mean "at the foot of the Dall river."

Near the ruin of the little church of Ardclinis at Red Bay is an unusual stream which flows down the face of the mountain and then dives into a natural tunnel where it continues underground until it reaches the sea. I wonder if this "blind" river does not have some connection with the name "Dall" — blind.

There was a foreigner once, Dallas by name, who was slain by Ossian of old. Some think the Dall river is named after him; others believe there is a connection with the Dall river being in fact the joining of two rivers, the Glenaan and Glenballyeamon. (Bun-an-daad).

At one time a landlord tried to change the name Cushendall to Newtownglens and for a time it appeared thus on maps and in the Parliamentary Gazetteer of Ireland. But the Glens people would have none of it, and luckily the beautiful old name is always now used. At one time it was also Bunandalla — the "bottom" (Bun) of the river Dall, but was changed to Cush (Cos) the "foot" of the river Dall.

The Hollow Sword Blade Company

Lands between Cushendun and Cushendall were in 1687 leased by the third Earl of Antrim to his illegitimate son, Daniel McDonnell, for a period of 500 years at the rent of £5 per annum. But after the defeat of James II Captain McDonnell departed to the Continent with the king and never returned, so his estates were forfeit.

The estate was purchased in 1702 by the Hollow Sword Blade Company for £2,596.

"This company was for making hollow sword blades. These swords had hollow backs in which quicksilver was put in order that, by rushing to the point, it might add an impetus to the blow." (O'Laverty).

The estate was later sold to various purchasers.

The Turnleys and Cushendall

In 1817 Mr. Francis Turnley cut a road round the ruins of Red Bay Castle to avoid the difficult road over the Crookanavick Hill to Cushendall. This was but one of the improvements carried out by this man, who came originally from Downpatrick in County Down, when he bought Cushendall in 1801.

Curfew Tower, Cushendall.

He also restored the old name from that of Newtownglens which had been inflicted by the previous owner on the inhabitants.

The Curfew Tower, built in 1809 as a barracks, was his pride and joy. He gave instructions that it was always to have a permanent garrison of one man who was not to leave it night or day. It was to be armed with one musket, a bayonet, a case of pistols and a pike 13 feet long. The guard was to ring the bell at 9 o'clock every night, the only time the bell was to be rung except as an alarm. Until recently the tower was occupied. Mr. Turnley died in 1845.

Along the main street there used to be a wee cinema where you could have had great crack with the neighbours before the show started. On past the churches and the quiet graveyard where so many of my friends and relatives lie and we are on the inland road to Ballycastle and Cushendun.

GLENAAN AND OSSIAN'S GRAVE

Just a short distance from Cushendall, on the left, we come to **Glenaan,** famed for **Ossian's Grave** in the place called Lubitavish, "loop of pleasure," on the Dall River.

> I'm dreamin' too, when the twilight chases
> The noise and clamour of toil away,
> Of the ash-crowned rath and the gentle places
> Where Finn and Ossian loved to stray;
> Of the thorn bush and of the fairy fountain
> Where the midnight moonbeams love to bide;
> Of the cairn high on the misty mountain,
> And the solemn calm of the countryside."

Glenaan has a quick river bubbling busily over boulders down the middle of the Glen. It is a bare and open glen; sort of honest, I always think.

Ossian's Grave, which can be described as a two-chambered horned cairn, can be found a little way up Glenaan, on the left. This is said to be the last resting-place of the warrior-poet of the third century, Ossian, a son of Finn Macool. The grave itself is much older than this, dating back to 2000 B.C.

Ossian

Who was **Ossian**? Ossian or Oisin was the son of Finn, leader of the Fianna, the bold band of heroes who fought, wandered, loved and sang in Ireland long ago. The Fianna were a brotherhood, and Ossian was not only one of their great warriors but also one of their greatest poets.

He himself had a brave warrior son, **Osgar,** who died tragically in a battle between the Fianna and the High King and his men. He was deeply lamented by both Finn and Oisin. For only twice did Finn shed tears — for Osgar and for his beloved dog **Bran**.

After this terrible battle and the loss of so many of their comrades the remainder of the Fianna were out hunting one day. Coming towards them was a beautiful girl on a white horse. She had long golden hair, blue eyes and cheeks redder than the rose. **Niamh of the Golden Head** was her name, daughter of the King of the Country of the Young. She said she had heard of the brave deeds of Oisin and had come to give him her love. Oisin was bewitched by her beauty and the pictures of the delightful country where she would take him. "O, pleasant golden-haired queen, you are my choice beyond the women of the world and I will go with you willingly."

So Oisin got on his horse, followed her to the strand and disappeared towards the sea. When his comrades saw this they gave three great shouts of lament. They would never see Oisin again.

After many years in the Country of the Young (some say "hundreds" though it seemed short to him) Oisin came back to Ireland and was found an old done man, lying on the ground. Saint Patrick had come to Ireland by then so he was carried to him. He stayed in Patrick's house and had long conversations with him, according to the old stories. Patrick tried to make a Christian of him but Oisin said, "I have no liking for clerks, their music is not sweet to me after his (Finn's).'' Patrick could not talk him out of his fretting and grieving for Finn and the days of the brave Fianna, all now gone.

Note (a):   The thigh bone of a man of a great stature was for a long time exhibited in the wall of the Old Layde Church, One of the giants of the Fianna perhaps?

Note (b):   (See Finn MacCool and the Dog Bran page 49).

Note (c):   An Account of Ossain's Grave is found in the Preliminary Survey of Ancient Monuments of Northern Ireland (1940) p. 19.

OSSIAN'S GRAVE, LUBITAVISH

They say
   It was here that Ossian died:
   I wonder if bright-haired Niamh cried?
   Whose lonely fingers piled the cairn
   And heaped it high with maiden fern?

They say
   That only the plovers know
   The feet that track the drifted snow,
   And the peeweets cry —
   Though they've never seen —
   The name of the one who loved Ossian.

I hope and I hope
   That he found somewhere
   His slender Niamh of the yellow hair,
   For theirs was a song too brief to scan
   With a rickle of bones
   And an old, blind man.

     Sydney Bell

GLENCORP

The road runs through this small glen on its way to Cushendun. It is a gentle place of small hill farms and whin-clad slopes gradually fading out to moorland on the rounded tops. A lonely ridge of trees on the skyline on the left used to tell I had almost reached my destination — my "Granny's in the Glens.''

THE SONG OF GLENDUN

Sure this is blessed Erin an' this the same glen,
The gold is on the whin-bush, the wather sings again,
The Fairy Thorn's in flower,—an' what ails my heart
   then?
        Flower o' the May,
        Flower o' the May,
What about the May time, an' he far away!

Summer loves the green glen, the white bird loves the sea,
An' the wind must kiss the heather top, and the red bell
   hides a bee;
As the bee is dear to the honeyflower, so one is dear to me.
        Flower o' the rose,
        Flower o' the rose,
A thorn pricked me one day, but nobody knows.

The bracken up the braeside has rusted in the air,
Three birches lean together, so silver limbed an' fair,
Och! golden leaves are flyin' fast, but the scarlet roan is
   rare.
        Berry o' the roan,
        Berry o' the roan,
The wind sighs among the trees, but I sigh alone.

I knit beside the turf fire, I spin upon the wheel,
Winter nights for thinkin' long, round runs the reel . . .
But he never knew, he never knew that here for him I'd
   kneel.
        Sparkle o' the fire,
        Sparkle o' the fire,
Mother Mary keep my love, an' send me my desire!

       Moira O'Neill

GLENDUN

"Lone Glendun of the wild glen flowers" was how Moira O'Neill described this steep-sided, well-wooded glen with its turf-brown (dun) river tumbling impulsively over its many boulders in the upper reaches and slowing to a lazy middle-aged spread on reaching the valley — a grand place for fishing when there's a flood on.

The hill farms here are approached by swaying bridges or by fording the river. Many bridges perished in a recent landslide and have been replaced by steel structures.

There, in the wee pool of Dunurgan, is the spot where old Murray spotted the fine big salmon when he went to get a bucket of water. He was a beauty but slippery — how to get him? The boyo lay flat on the grass, made a dive with his head, caught the salmon with his teeth and landed him! A bang with a stone did the rest.

There was a pool higher up, where some of the poachers tried dynamite; a cruel way to go about the job, I thought.

Past the white-washed chapel and Craigagh Wood with its "Altar in the Woods" the Dun river glides under the old arched bridge to blend with the sea at Cushendun.

The Altar in the Woods

Here is a very ancient stone with a carving of a crucifix and a winged cherub above it. The stone was brought from Scotland to use as an altar by Catholics in the days of the Penal Laws. The people used to meet for worship under an old oak, but wanted a special stone — a "good" stone — to mark the meeting place. Some men from the glens rowed over to Scotland and brought this one back. It may be from Iona.

Although there is a fine chapel nearby, every year in the month of June many people come to pray at the old altar.

Nearby in the little churchyard is another very curious stone.

The Stone In Craigagh Churchyard

This stone marks the burial place of Charles McAllister, shipmate of Nelson for 22 years, who died at the ripe old

E

age of 97. It seemed that Charles McAllister and Horatio Nelson had as boys been shipmates on the "Carcass." Later they were together at the Battle of the Baltic. Nelson was feeling depressed: "Charlie, I doubt it's all up with us." Charlie replied "Houl' your tongue; rake your guns and you'll be all right." The advice was taken, and the battle won.

There is a crude drawing on the tombstone of a little ship anchored at both ends, with the inscription "Your ship, love, is moored head and stern for a fuldiew." Some say the ship is to remind us of the ship-of-war in which McAllister sailed with Nelson; others say it is the lower left quartering of the McAllister arms, which quartering is the same as that of the McDonnells.

There is also on the stone a rough carving of something resembling a goat. Some believe this represents McAllister as a "scapegoat."

The late Mr. Sam Henry, folklorist, found that when a ship was laid up for any reason the sailors received all leave that had accrued during the voyage — a "full due" leave. In this case the leave was for eternity.

It is said that when Nelson was parting with his friend, Charles, he offered him a choice of three things: he might have a permit of freedom from curfew restrictions; he might save a man from the gallows, or he might receive 50 guineas in cash. Charles took the cash and let the credit go!

Seanan's Isle In the River Near Glendun Church

There is a story in the Tripartite Life that St. Patrick was displeased with St. Olcan over a certain matter of disobedience and he, Patrick, said that Oican's lands (Innispollan?) would be given to St. MacNissi and to Seanan of Innis Altic (the island of birds). O'Laverty equates Innispollan with Innis Altic. Seanan was a Bishop in this part of North Antrim. So the Saint himself may have had a direct connection with the church in this area.

This song from the 18th century, about an exile's longing for home, was originally sung in Irish.

I believe it refers to the townland of Ardicoan, near Glendun. Another translation, called The Quiet Land of Erin, is sung by Mary O'Hara.

AIRD A' CHUMHAING

If I were in Aird a' Chumhaing,
Near the mountain that is far from me,
I would seldom be without paying a visit
To the*Glen of the Cuckoo on Sunday.

>Agus, och, och, Eire—agus O!
>Sorrow to me—and Oh!
>It is my heart that is heavy, sad.

It is many a Christmas I myself would be
In Cushendun and I all alone,
Playing on the white strand
And my hurley stick in my hand.

Am I not weary here by myself
Without hearing the voices of the woodcock, blackbird or
  corncrake?
Sparrow, thrush, snipe itself,
And without knowing Sunday itself!

This is the twisting that is lasting;
To put such a (deception) on the world;
To entice the sheep from the lamb -
And to entice my youth from me.

If I had a skiff and oars
I would take myself off on the ridge of the waves,
And I swear to God I would reach health,
And I would die in Erin.

S. MacAmbrois (McCambridge)

(Translation by Sydney Bell)

Note: *Glendun has also been known as the Glen of the Cuckoo.

CUSHENDUN

This little village, now under the care of the National Trust, was once described by St. John Irvine as the loveliest village in the world. Cushendun is **Bun-abhann-Duine** in the Annals of the Four Masters. It was afterwards changed to **Cois-abhann-Duine** which has been gradually compressed to the present name meaning "the foot of the Dun River." It is the nearest Irish port to Britain.

According to the Rev. Mr. Dobbs, writing in the early 19th century, Cushendun used to be a busy little port with constant traffic between it and the Mull of Kintyre, sending over black cattle and pigs and returning with Highland ponies.*

Cushendun is modelled on a Cornish-style village. It is beloved of painters and poets, this place where "the blue lips of the sea reach for the amber bowl of the land."

The little beach at Cushendun is quite pebbly and I have spent many hours here looking for "precious" stones. I have seen some beautifully-cut polished stones from this beach. Here, too, the local farmers drew many a load of stones and sand for their various needs.

The caves at the back of the hotels are quite famous and unusual. They are of sandstone conglomerate, and they make quite an eerie entrance to "Cave House" which lies beyond. In Mr. Crommelin's time he had "store-rooms here, a powder magazine, a smith's forge and a cow-house." The poet John Masefield won his bride at this spot, and he says.

"In the curlew-calling time of Irish dusk
Life became more splendid than its husk."

Moira O'Neill is, of course, the poet of the Glens whose poems have been famous for over 60 years. She was born in the large square white house by the bay. Her name was Nesta Higginson. She lived in Canada after her marriage but eventually returned to live in the South of Ireland. Her sensitive poems of the beauty of the Glens and the way of life of the people are still a delight.

The Brabla Burn featured in several of Moira O'Neill's poems bubbles down the hill near Milltown, a cluster of houses behind Cushendun Bay.

Note: *Ailsa Craig, the huge rock near the Ayrshire coast, is known as Paddy's Milestone.

CUTTIN' RUSHES

Oh maybe it was yesterday, or fifty years ago!
Meself was risin' early on a day for cuttin' rushes,
Walkin' up the Brabla' burn, still the sun was low,
Now I'd hear the burn run an' then I'd hear the thrushes.
Young, still young!—an' drenchin' wet the grass,
Wet the golden honeysuckle hangin' sweetly down;
Here, lad, here! will ye follow where I pass,
An' find me cuttin' rushes on the mountain.

Then was it only yesterday, or fifty years or so?
Rippin' round the bog pools high among the heather,
The hook it made me hand sore, I had to leave it go,
'Twas he that cut the rushes then for me to bind together.
Come, dear, come!—an' back along the burn
See the darlin' honeysuckle hangin' like a crown.
Quick, one kiss,—sure, there's someone at the turn!
Oh, we're afther cuttin' rushes on the mountain.

Moira O'Neill

GRACE FOR LIGHT

When we were little childer we had a quare wee house,
Away up in the heather by the head o' Brabla burn;
The hares we'd see them scooting, an' we'd hear the
    crowin' grouse
An' when we'd all be in at night ye'd not get room to turn.

The youngest two She'd put to bed, their faces to the wall.
An' the lave of us could sit aroun', just anywhere we
    might;
Herself would take the rush-dip an' light it for us all,
An "God be thanked!" she would say,—"now we have a
    light.

Then we be to quet the laughin' an' pushin' on the floor,
An' think on One who called us to come and be forgiven;
Himself 'ud put his pipe down, an' say the good word more,
"May the Lamb o' God lead us all to the Light o' Heaven!"

There'a wheen things that used to be an' now has had their
    day,
The Nine Glens of Antrim can show ye many a sight;
But not the quare wee house where we lived up Brabla
    way,
Nor a child in all the nine Glens that knows the grace for
    light.

Moira O'Neill

John o' the Rocks' wee low cottage on the other side of the bay is a favourite spot with painters. This John was given "o' the Rocks" as a nickname to distinguish him from others of the same name. (McNeills).

On the steep road which leads to Torr Head is the cairn erected to the memory of Shane O'Neill, Shane the Proud.

The Torr Road And Shane O'Neill's Monument

Shane O'Neill was murdered at Carra Castle, near Cushendun, in 1567 by the McDonnells with whom he had unwisely taken refuge. After supper a fight started and O'Neill fell as a result of many wounds.

"His body was wrapped in a soldier's old shirt and flung into a pit in an old chapel; his head was cut off and taken to Dublin in order that the offered reward might be claimed from the Government there. It was a pathetic end for one known as Sean the Proud. The churchyard of his unseemly burial is in Ballyteerim townland and is known as Cross Shreen." (Dr. D. A. Chart — A history of Northern Ireland).

A monument in the form of a cairn, in memory of Shane O'Neill, has been erected high on the hillside above Cushendun. This is also a monument to Roger Casement and other Irish patriots.

Between Torr and Cushendun is the road known as "the road Lady Londonderry (Frances Anne) was wrecked on". Her ladyship had set out for a drive in her coach and four with her new English coachman at the reins. Past Cushendun the road became more and more difficult and dangerous so Lady Londonderry decided to turn, but this was impossible as the track was so narrow two carts could not even pass. Eventually the horses were taken out and an army of labourers summoned and gradually they persuaded the coach to face the direction required. They returned thankfully to Cushendun.

There is another difficult road here known as the "Corkscrew Road" which climbs from Cushendun in a series of sharp zig-zags to join the road to Ballycastle from Cushendall.

Torr Road with its majestic views of cliff and sea and lovely bays is a delight, but it is twisty and steep and needs a careful driver. Torr Head is a magnificent cone, the nearest point to Scotland. Here, too, great fires were lit by the Antrim Scots when they needed help from their kinsmen in Scotland.

TORR

Around Torr are several interesting historical remains.
In Torr West, a short distance from the road between
Ballycastle and Torr, are scattered standing stones called
the Meurogs, the "finger" stones, supposed to have been
thrown from Torr Head by a giant!

A short distance west of the Meurogs lies St. Columba's
Stone, " **a rude stone 3 feet long and 1 foot thick having on
its flat side some indentations said to be the impressions of
the hand and foot of the Saint."** (O'Laverty).

On the great headland of Torr was a fort called the Fort
of Barach*(Dun Bharaigh). Barach is the giant who is
reputed to have flung the Finger Stones at the other five
giants near Ballyucan with whom he was having a bit of a
fight!

SLAINTE! CUSHLAKE

Slainte! Cushlake, methinks I hear
The fisherman's anthem once again
Ring round the headlands wild and clear,
The cheery ring of the old refrain,
Oft as it echoed round by Torr
Oft as it run o'er cliff and hollow,
Oft as it sounded round that shore,
Slainte, Cushlake, O baile go baile!*

Oh! for the short, sweet summer night,
When the leaves are green on the woods of Clona;
Oh! for the wild waves leaping white
O'er the long bleak point of Tornamona;
Oh! for a good seaworthy craft,
The sails well set, and the wind to follow;
The dark green breakers foaming abaft,
Then Slainte, Cushlake, O baile go baile!

Though I may ne'er again behold
The sunset glow on old Kintyre,
Tinging the rugged cliffs with gold,
Till all the headlands seem on fire,
Though I on Ailsa Craig no more,
May see it gleam like a rosy hollow,
Or shine on Sanda's distant shore,
Yet, Slainte, Cushlake, O baile go baile!

Dusty Rhodes

Note: *This Barach is the one involved in the sad story of the Sons of
Usnach (see Ballycastle). Cassinbarrow nearby is the path of Barach,
and Slaght Baragh is the monument of Barach where we assume he
is buried.

Note: *This greeting may be translated: "A health to Cushlake from wall to
wall." Cushlake is the mountain area from Cushendun to Torr Head.

MURLOUGH

Murlough Bay is a beautiful, deep-set crescent where gentle woods edge the sea, and until recently it was inaccessible to the motorist. It has been opened up by the National Trust and many more can now enjoy this beauty. Here Roger Casement asked to be buried, but it could not be. A plain Celtic cross looks to the sea in his memory.

A Saint Mologe is associated with Murlough, and at one time his grave was well known, but today he and his origins are rather hard to trace. A special mass, called the "Fair of Murlough," was once held there. It is thought that Mo and Oge were added to the name "Luan," a saint from Bangor who founded many monasteries. A church called Kilvoruan in Rathlin is associated with him.

Note: The road from Torr joins the main Ballycastle Road at Ballyvoy.
Note: Murlough is also in Irish Mur-bholg, the "sea-inlet."

Other Roads From Cushendall

On this journey we left Cushendall by the main road to Cushendun. Two other delightful winding roads explore the land between Cushendall and Cushendun. The middle road, a continuation of the steep road up behind the Curfew Tower, passes the old Fair Green, scene of some of the famous old Cushendall fairs. This road skirts **Tiveragh**, the "fairy hill." An eye-witness describes his eerie experiences here in another section. (see page 81)

ON TIV-RA HILL

On Tiv-ra Hill near Cushendall,
I heard a commotion behind a wall.
I stopped and looked over, and boys-o-boys!
Now what do you think was makin' the noise?

'Twas a hurley match—and may I choke —
It was two wee teams of the Fairy-folk
That was ripplin' and tearing' and weltin' away
In the light of the moon that was bright as the day.

And their playing-pitch was hardly as big
As my Uncle Barney's potato rig;
And me there watchin' them puck and clout —
At the back o' the wall with my eyes stuck out.

When all at once, like the squeal of a hare,
A wee voice shouted, "Who's that up there?"
And a bit of a thing about nine-inch tall
Came climbing up to the top of the wall.

And he stood there, he stood about pot-size
With his two wee fingers up at my eyes,
And it's God's own truth that I'm speakin' mind ye,
"Get out o' that," says he, "or I'll blind ye!"

Aye that's what he said, "I'll blind ye," says he,
And by Jing what he said was enough for me.
Did I run? Aye surely; I didn't miss —
And I haven't seen Tiv-ra from that to this.

H. Browne

There is a very long saga by Dusty Rhodes about the blacksmith called Robert Kennedy who lived near Tivera.

Here are some of the verses.

ROBERT KENNEDY — A TALE OF 1798

Come hither for a shanagh, come hither, Shawn agrah.
Do you remember Kennedy, the smith of Tiev-a raw?
Can I forget, ma bouchal, the ancient man replied,
The hero who so often fought for Erin by my side?

A braver heart there was not found in all the rebel ranks,
When nightly they assembled on Dalla's mossy banks;
A hero true and staunch was he as ever took the field,
For the gleaming blade himself had made right well his
    arm could wield.

F

And seldom near the smithy was Robin to be seen,
Except when pikes were wanted by the boys that loved the
green;
An outlawed man was he from social pleasure barred;
His bed the slopes of Trostan or the cave of steep Barrard.

But hark! a sound disturbs the air, a sound the peasants
dread,
'Tis the clanking of the sabre and the yeoman's steady
tread;
What brings them here from Cushendall this summer
evening, say,
They're out tonight to seek the life of Robin Kennedy.

The smith threw off his apron, and flung his hammer
down,
Then darting from the smithy door, dashed through the
heather brown;
He paused not for an instant, but onward swiftly pressed,
To seek a place of safety on Aura's distant crest.

The night is fast approaching, but still the hunted man
Sped onward, ever onward, through the valley of Glenaan;
Close, close behind, the Yeomen ride and bright their
sabres gleam
God help you Robert Kennedy your danger is extreme.

He led them on by hill and bawn till midnight's dreary
hour,
Past many a rugged boreen and many a thorny bower,
Until he gained a deep morass, a dark and treacherous
mere;
They'll wet their feet, said Kennedy, who come to seek me
here.

At length the weary Captain, his midnight search in vain,
From Aura's dreary mountain reluctant turned his rein;
Through deep Glendun, past Eagle Hill, 'mong,
Esheragh's boulders grey
The spot was never found where the rebel blacksmith lay.

And there he lay till dawn of day gleamed in the eastern
sky
When on the far horizon a flame shot fierce and high;
He knew they'd fired his cottage, but Robin did not mind —
They've burnt the cage, said Kennedy, the bird they
cannot find.

They set a price upon his head, they searched the country
   round
From Torr to Ballyemon Glen, but Robin was not found;
They searched for many a weary day by Tiev-a raw's
   green brae
But they never found the rebel smith, brave Robin Kennedy.

This middle road with its feathery beech trees winds on
to meet the main Cushendun Road near **Dunurgan,** and
we look down on the gentle farms of **Glencorp** and the
splendid beauties of mountain and glen. It is the "old
road" of my childhood, where we roamed free as birds but
keeping grandfather's white-washed house in view as
"base-camp."

LAYDE

The road to the right at the Curfew Tower leads to the
sea at **Cushendall** but just before coming to the bay there is
a road which bears left over the hill. It is the way to Layde,
climbing high above lovely **Red Bay** and its confining hills.

The famous old **Layde Churchyard,** burying place of the
Macdonnells, should not be missed.

A quiet mossy lane leads to this hallowed place in a little
glen set high above the sea. Here is an uncanny quiet. It is
unbelievably cool, even on a hot summer's day. All around
are tumbled ancient gravestones dominated by the fine
Celtic cross to the memory of Dr. James McDonnell, a
descendant of the famous McDonnells or Macdonnells of
the Glens. The cross is decorated with biblical stories of
healing, with entwined Celtic spirals. The inscription
shows a man respected and loved.

**"He was a man beloved whose ability was ever out-
weighed by his piety."** He had been a patron of the old Irish
harpers and kept open house for some of them, and was
one of the first medical men to operate under chloroform.

The MacDonnells

This old graveyard was the burying place of the senior
branch of the MacDonnells, the descendants of Colla, of
Kinbane Castle, elder brother of Sorley Boy.

A direct descendant of Sorley Boy told me about a curious whinstone in the old churchyard. She says it has on it a device of the Patron Saint of the clan. Would this be St. Kieran? The coat of arms on several of the gravestones is that of the MacDonnells—the salmon, the deer, the lymphad, the hand grasping the cross-crosslet.

Layde was once the site of a Franciscan monastery, and the church was in regular use until 1790 when services were transferred to a house called "The Old Inn" in Cushendall, and later to the new Layde Parish Church.

An old MS states **"In a dell near the shore, about one mile from Cushendall, are the ruins of a small religious house, said to have been founded by the sept McFall or McFaul."**

Saint Kieran of Clonmacnoise was the Patron Saint of the church. A well close to the road above Layde church is called St. Kieran's Well. The surname McIlheron or McElheran is Mac Gilla-Ciaran, descendant of the disciple or servant of Kieran.

This Irish Saint went to Scotland in the 7th century and dwelt in a cave near Campbelltown (old local name being Ceann-loch-cill-Ciaran), so called for the Saint's original church built at the head of Campbelltown Bay. In the Episcopal Church of Scotland the present church at Campbelltown is dedicated to St. Kieran.

Note: There was a church first built near the Fair Hill. But this was not suitable and in 1830 the present Layde Parish Church was built.

The Three McArthurs

From 1696 to 1793 three generations of Protestant clergy served at Layde, father, son and grandson. They resided at Tromra.* At this time Irish was the predominant tongue in the Glens, and these three clergymen preached to their people in their own language.

At **Castlegreen*** we bear left up over the mountain, or up "the line," as we called the Ballycastle Road. This road that spans lovely **Glendun** and its river by way of the famous viaduct (our "big bridge") is one of the loveliest I know.

Note: *Tromra, place of the "boor" tree or elder).
Note: *Castlegreen (see page 75).

On all sides the boggy moorland, purple and brown, with its bright green patches of grass and waving bog-cotton, is a delight to the eye and an invitation to roam.

Cutting the turf.

Nor is there a monotonous flatness to the moor. Giant grey boulders left by some ancient glacier lie grouped in elegant abandon. Turf stacks with their precise, regular shapes break the skyline, a tribute to man's industry and artistry.

Sheep are everywhere; on the road, too, if it suits them. The curlew and the seagulls call and swirl. The air is bracing, sharp with winter chill or balmy when summer blazes down on the brittle turf. Among the stones the hidden springs bubble with sweet water for the thirsty worker.

Scattered stones of abandoned farmsteads add a sad postscript to this road. To wrest a living from the stubborn earth became just too hard.

MY SORROW IT IS

(Written at one such homestead looking down on Cushendun)

My sorrow it is this day
That the tongue of the Glens is dead!
My sorrow to hear them say
That the light of the Glens has fled.

No smooring of fires this night!
No telling of tales! No song!
Not a song or a Grace for Light
The length of the Glens along.

Where once there was laughter and fun;
Where once there was dancing go leor,
There is only the light of the sun
To streak the deserted floor.

Accusing, the gables stand
By the fuchsias running wild,
And in all the length of the land
There is never a barefoot child

With the liquid tongue of his sires
To lilt me a song this night;
Or women to smoor the fires,
And murmur the Grace for Light.

Sydney Bell

LOUGHAREEMA

Loughareema, the "Vanishing Lake" or "Fairy Lough,"
on either side of the Ballycastle Road, is known to most
travellers. It can be full of water one day, almost flooding
the road; the next it could be empty, the water having
drained away through the underlying layer of chalk.
"But where do the fish go?" we used to ask.
"Down the holes. They come and go with the water."
It is the only explanation, when you come to think of it.
Moira O'Neill loved this place and made it famous in her
poetry.

Loughareema! Loughareema
Lies so high among the heather;
A little lough, a dark lough,
The wather's black an' deep.
Ould herons go a-fishing there,
An' sea-gulls all together.
Float roun' the one green island
On the fairy lough asleep.

But there was danger here as well as beauty. A man
called McNeill perished when carriage and horses plunged
into the Lough.

Ballypatrick Forest, looming up on both sides of the
road, brings us back abruptly to man and his need for work
and wealth. The moorland vistas are shut out and
regretfully we begin to descend.
But soon we see the lovely valley of the Carey river on
our left. (Carey—Cathair-Riog), the king's chair. This
area could once have belonged to an important chief, as all
round there is evidence of a storied past with souterrains,
dolmens and duns.

At the end of the mountain road we arrive at the tiny village of **Ballyvoy** and the shoreward road to the right that leads to Torr. Joseph Campbell, the poet, described this area in his "The Golden Hills of Ballyucan."

"And down from Cuil-na-gcopog, Gleann-seisg, and Croc-an-air,
A hundred silver streamlets danced before the dawning fire,
And the mottled thrushes in the trees sang songs of deep desire
To the golden hills of Baile-eocain O!"

We come suddenly to **Culfeightrin** and its little church. Culfeightrin, "the corner of the stranger," is where St. Patrick founded a church and left St. Fiachtrach in charge. Then the great mound of Knocklayd soars up on our left shadowing Ballycastle and our last two glens which lie on either side of the mountain, **Glenshesk** and **Glen Taisie** or **Glentow.**

Corrymeela

A road to the right has the pointer **"Corrymeela"** leading to a community centre for the reconciliation of the people of Ulster. The name means "hill of harmony." Moira O'Neill's **Corrymeela** was a little further round the coast near Cushendun:

Over here in England I'm helpin' wi' the hay,
An' wisht I was in Ireland the livelong day;
Weary on the English hay, an' sorra take the wheat!
Och! Corrymeela an' the blue sky over it.

There's a deep dumb river flowin' by beyont the heavy trees,
This livin' air is moithered wi' the hummin' o' the bees;
I wisht I'd hear the Claddagh burn go runnin' through the heat.
Past Corrymeela, wi' the blue sky over it.

Moira O'Neill

KNOCKLAYD

Knocklayd is said to have been called after Fergus MacLiede, a warrior of old.

There is another story about a Scottish girl Lydia who eloped with a young man and landed on a rock in the townland of Layd. Later she fled to Knocklayd giving her name to both places.

"People rave of the scenery out in the West
And they say of all lands 'tis the fairest and best
But they don't know the talent Dame Nature displayed
When she last touched her canvas and painted Knocklayd."

Knocklayd was once known as **Dunlayd,** and from ancient records it would appear that the name Layd was given to a very extensive tract of this part of Antrim. Perhaps it was the old name for **Dalriada** before the Cairbre-Riada conquered these parts.

On the summit are the ruins of a cairn, "the cairn of the three." One legend has it that three Norwegians are buried there, while another says it marks the grave of a Scottish lady called McLeod and her two children.

I think that Fergus MacLiede is most likely to be the one to have given his name to the mountain.

Note: **Knocklayd** (Choc leithid), the broad hill, rises to 1,695 feet.

GLENSHESK

Just as you come into Ballycastle over the bridge there is a road to the left, leading to **Glenshesk**, a V-shaped, well-wooded glen. Glenshesk is wild and unspoiled, with a lovely forest park and picnic area nearby. There are splendid views here of **Rathlin** and the **Mull of Kintyre.**

One of the fascinating things to see in the townland of Carnsumpson is **Doonfin,** a little knoll or rath where Finn Macool's dog died. It is said that Finn tried to console himself by composing lamentations, and in an account from Mason's Parochial Survey (1816) a curious Irish heroic poem is described, the manuscript being owned by one Charles McIldowney. An old chaunt of six notes, the first four low and solemn and the concluding two loud and rapid, used to be known by the inhabitants of Ramoan.

FINN MacCOUL AND THE DOG BRAN

As Finn MacCoul went hunting
One summer's afternoon
In dark Glenshesk's deep valley,
Beneath the silvery moon,

His good dog Bran before the rest
Fast on the red deer came,
The bravest dog that ever ran,
A hound of ancient fame.

He soon o'er took the flying deer,
And pulled the quarry down,
Slaying another of the herd,
To add to his renown,

Returning to his master
He soon appeared in view,
His gory jaws were open wide,
From which the foam flecks flew.

Now Finn MacCoul was sore afraid,
When thus the dog he saw
Fast bounding to his master's side,
Blood dripping from his jaw.

He placed an arrow in the bow,
And fast the string he drew,
And by a true and well-aimed shaft
His faithful hound he slew.

Now Finn was wild because he slew
His faithful greyhound so,
Though when the dog appeared in view
His fate he did not know

And from that day brave Finn became,
A sad and altered man,
Still crying, "A mauvroun, I've slain
My faithful servant Bran.

Dusty Rhodes

G

In among the woods on the slopes of Knocklayd are the ruins of an ancient church known as the Goban Saer's* Castle. There is a round tower in the grounds of the Church at Armoy, at one end of Glenshesk.

Note: *The Goban Saer in Irish folklore was the builder of many ancient structures including the round towers.

THE BUACHALAN BWEE

"As I walked by the salmon stream in the sea-sounding valley of Glenshesc on a day of soft rain, with the Blue Hills of Antrim around me, and I sad and lonely, there came a strange happening. The Buachalan Bwee stirred at a sudden calling, and I saw very plainly they were not flowers at all, but soldiers each in his saffron line, waiting silently."

Though all along the valley
The golden Soldiers stand,
There is no sound of marching
Through MacEsmund's land.

No flashing of the claymore
From Glenshesc to the sea;
In their hosts of green and amber
They keep watch silently.

Do the sorrow Sons of Usnach
Thrall them beyond the seas,
Till Naoisi comes a-sailing
Past the lonely Hebrides?

Will Cuchulainn, dark and star-like,
Flame in splendour north and south,
And woo their souls from slumber
By the thunder of his mouth?

They guard the Peace of Enan
Round Drumsenie's place of prayer,
Yet not for him or Colum
Do they toss their yellow hair.

If they made no tryst with Patraic,
They kissed him, brow and chin;
When down the flock-filled valley
His feet came wanderin'.

Once in the days of Lammas,
I heard him wake again;
Sorley Boy MacDonaill
Calling through the rain:

As sighs the purple heather,
From Trostan to Cnoclaid;
Each in his tent of hill-mist,
Stirred at the caoine he made.

As sweeps the long sun-shadows
On Eachra's jewelled rim,
By Mairge and by Carey,
They turned and followed him.

Now along the valley,
They lift their gilded shields;
In countryside and townland,
Lords of the pasture fields.

But oh! that I had followed,
When his cry rang up the glen,
Sorley Boy MacDonaill
And his Golden Soldier-men!''

Florence Wilson

The Buachalan Bwee is the ben-weed or ragwort.

GLENTAISIE

Glentaisie, or **Glentow,** which lies on the western side of
Knocklayd, is a small glen through which the main road
runs from **Ballycastle** to **Armoy.** Compared with the wild
sweeps of the other glens it is tucked in, sensible and
domesticated. The name **Taisie** is associated with a
princess of Rathlin, and here she gloried in a great battle.
But Tow is still a mystery to me, unless it is just named
after the river Tow.   (See page 92 for Taisie's story.)

And so we have wandered from glen to glen, nine in all,
having a look, admiring a view, thrilling to grandeur and
wild beauty. Each glen is different—sad, happy, open,
secret, wild, cosy. Each has its own stories, poems, songs
and legends.

We have just got to know them all in this section: now we
can go deeper and make friends with the Glens, the
Glensfolk and their ways.

THE WITCH OF GLENTOW

Near a high thorn hedge by the side of the way,
In a cottage a woman of eighty did stay;
Though few of the people remember her now,
Then everyone knew the old witch of Glentow.

She came to the country, and none knew from where:
By the side of the river she planted herself there,
A conical bonnet adorned her brow,
And everyone feared the old witch of Glentow.

A woman refused to supply her a meal;
Full quickly that woman her vengeance did feel —
Two sheep disappeared from the farm somehow;
All said they were slain by the witch of Glentow.

Though no one would venture to do the hag harm,
Yet all round they suffered on every farm;
The butter was ta'en from the milk of the cow.
As everyone said by the witch of Glentow.

Two young fellows swore that the witch they would slay,
So one night to the seashore they bore her away,
And then flung her into the breakers somehow,
'Twas thus that they drowned the witch of Glentow.

So, now after nightfall her voice they can hear,
Her eerie moans filling the bosom with fear,
By the side of the river she wanders somehow,
Where you'll hear the dread cry of the witch of Glentow.

Ere a year both the young men from life passed away,
Though the means of their death now there's no one can
    say;
But now from the river's deep shadow I vow
The people oft hear the old witch of Glentow.

Dusty Rhodes

Knocklayd.

Glentaisie of the fairy songs;
Glenshesk of the brown burns;
Glendun that stirs from her sleep while you pass;
Glenariff of the leaping waterfalls and silver bir-
    ches;
Glencorp whose name forbids us calling there;
Glenballyeamon like a battler's queen
When her pulse at his pibroch thrills;
Glengorm — the blue glen;
Glencloy — the glen of shadows;
And Glenaan — the glen of the fuchsias and the little
    ford.

Joseph Campbell

BUN-NA-MARGY

Bun-na-Margy is the name of the old monastery to be seen on the left as one approaches Ballycastle. The name means "the foot of the Margy", the river formed by the joining of the Shesk and Carey rivers.

The monastery is said to have been founded by Rory MacQuillan, Lord of the Route, about the year 1500, but another tale says it was erected as an act of atonement by Phelim McCormick who had committed murder. The Franciscans were installed.

It is believed that the first battle between the Mac-Donnells and MacQuillans was fought on land adjacent to the monastery.

Colla MacDonnell is probably buried at Bun-na-Margy and other MacDonnells, too, though Layde is also a MacDonnell burying place. Four Earls and Marquesses of Antrim are buried there with their wives. The ruins are worth visiting. The church measures 99 feet by 24½ feet and there are several interesting carvings to be seen. At the west end is a small primitive cross believed to mark the burying place of Julia MacQuillan, the Black Nun of Bun-na-Margy.

The Black Nun was, it seems, a great prophetess and much revered in her life-time. One of her prophecies was that **Knocklayd** would bring forth a great torrent of water which would inundate the country for seven miles around. At her death she was interred at the door of the chapel as had been her wish so that she might be trodden under the feet of those who entered.

Dunaneenie Castle (Fort of the Fairs) was built by Alexander MacIan Cathanac Macdonnell who fled to the Glens about 1500 from trouble in Scotland. He was Lord of Islay, Kintyre, and the Glens, being a direct descendant of John, Lord of the Isles, who in 1399 married Marjorie, the Bissett heiress of the Glens.

Kinbane Castle (the White Head) was built by Alexander's third son, Colla. It was probably here he brought his wife Eveleen Maquillan. Then his quarrels with the Maquillans began.

Dunamallact (Fort of the Curse) has an interesting story attached to it. It seems that Donnell Malacht was the sixth son of Alexander, Lord of the Isles. His mother, when carrying this child, cursed it as her husband had killed her five brothers in battle, all in one day. Her prayer was that, if she had a daughter, she would be a harlot; if a son, he would never see the light of day. It is said that her prayer was answered.

Dunnamallacht lies just behind Sheskburn House, in Ballycastle.

The Grey Man's Path.

FAIR HEAD

This great headland at the far end of the bay is sometimes called **Benmore**. A curious story gave it the name **Fair Head**.

In a castle on **Rathlin** lived a beautiful girl. She had many suitors, but two of them were so keen for her hand that they started a fight. It was agreed that the winner would marry the girl. One of them was mortally wounded, and with his dying breath he whispered to his servant, Thol Dhu, to dance with the girl out on the cliffs that were below the castle. Thol Dhu obeyed his master, and began to dance. They danced nearer and nearer the edge until over they whirled, the faithful servant losing his own life to avenge his master.

Now the spot on the mainland where her body was washed up was from then on known as **Fair Head** because of the beautiful yellow hair of the drowned girl.

On the headland is the **Grey Man's Path.** This was supposed to be named after a holy man who came here each day for prayer and meditation. Legend has given him a more sinister role. He is a ghost that brings bad luck to whoever sees him.

Note: Fair Head is mentioned as Robogdunum, the fort of Robog, a legendary giant, by Ptolemy the first century geographer.

The name of the townland, Ballyucan, near Fair Head is said to derive from Bally-jotun "the habitation of the jotuns or Nordic Giants." On the edge of Fair Head rests a stone known as Finn MacCoul's Finger Stone, which Finn is said to have thrown from Rathlin to scare away a cow that was grazing too near the edge.

The Grey Man has been associated with An Fir Lea, the storm-god of the Danaan race 1500 B.C. and was indeed believed in by other races of the Middle East. His name, An Fir Lea, can be seen around this coast in Portnoffer at the Giant's Causeway, Stack-an-Var-lea on Rathlin, and, of course, Cassan-firlea, the Grey Man's Path.

A path used by dulse-gatherers on the Murlough side of Fair Head is called **Kishla.**

The Enchanted Prince

Mary McAnulty was an old woman who made her living gathering dulse below Fair Head. As she always used the entrance to the Grey Man's Path, it came to be known as Mary McAnulty's Hall Door. One evening when she was returning home with a bag of dulse on her back and it near dusk, she met a fine gentleman near her "hall door". He walked with her to a place not far from Lough Dhu, where she sat down to rest. The stranger then spoke to her. He asked her to look at his hair and tell what she saw. She said "It's green". "And no wonder", said he, "for I have lived for years under that Black Lough".

They walked on a bit and again sat down to rest. This time he put his head on her lap and went to sleep. Then Mary noticed his cloven hoof and she became alarmed. She slipped away and left him sleeping. But when he awoke and found his companion gone this enchanted prince changed into a horse and let out of him such great neighs that he frightened the whole townland. But Mary had escaped, and we suppose the queer horse-man returned to his dwelling in Lough Dhu.

This is, in fact, the old Celtic legend of An Each-Uisge, or water-horse, told in other Celtic lands.

Wandering over this headland is a herd of wild goats. Long may they have peace to be truly "wild".

The **Rock of Usnach** is the name given to a large flat rock lying near the foot of the great headland.

DEIRDRE AND THE SONS
OF USNACH

There was once a harper to King Conchubar of Ireland who had one child, a daughter Deirdre. A druid had foretold she was to be the most beautiful girl to be found in Ireland but that, because of this gift of beauty, trouble, sorrow and bloodshed would be caused among many.

In an attempt to avoid this, her father sent her to be brought up by a foster mother in a hut in a remote place. Food was brought to them but Deirdre was to see no one from the outside world and thus she was sheltered until she was fourteen. But then a hunter lost his way one night and arrived looking for hospitality at the hut. It was reluctantly given by the foster mother for she knew the secret of the presence of the girl would now be out. The hunter was amazed by the girl's beauty and planned to tell the King, thinking her to be a fit wife for Conchubar of Emain Macha (Armagh).

The King decided to go and see her for himself. He fell in love with her and wished to marry her at once. But she begged for a year and a day to prepare herself for her great duties when she would be a king's wife. This was granted.

Meanwhile, Deirdre one day caught sight of three of the noblest young men in Ireland, the Sons of Usnach—Naoise, Ainnle and Ardan—singing as they went. She was fascinated by them and fell in love with Naoise who had his head and shoulders above all the men of Ireland. He returned her love, and thus protected by the three brothers Deirdre fled with them. Eventually they came to Scotland and gave their help to the King of Scotland. But the King of Scotland too tried to get Deirdre for himself; so finally she and the three brothers moved to a very lonely place to live in peace.

Meanwhile King Conchubar said at a great feast that he missed the Sons of Usnach and wondered if he should ask them back. Who would take the message? His words were sweet, but there was no forgiveness in his heart. He sent Fergus for them after Fergus made a promise not to harm the King if, by chance, some evil should befall the Sons of Usnach.

The King made Fergus also promise to send the Sons of Usnach and Deirdre to him at Armagh, immediately they arrived in Ireland. But he also told Fergus to call at the

H

Dun of Borach first. With this Borach the King arranged for a great feast to be prepared which Fergus could not under oath refuse.

Fergus went to Scotland with his own two sons. Deirdre was very troubled by Fergus's arrival, and full of terrible premonitions about returning to Ireland, but Naoise wished to return and brushed aside her fears.

On the way back to Ireland Deirdre wished to stay in Rathlin but again Naoise would not listen, and on the Rock of Usnach they landed in Ireland.

But Borach greeted them with his feast prepared. Fergus was in a dilemma: he wanted to protect the four he had brought to Ireland but was under geis (a solemn oath) to accept the hospitality. He stayed to feast, and sent his two sons on with the party to protect them.

Alas, Fergus was betrayed. One of his sons tried to help, but the other was bribed. The Sons of Usnach were murdered at Armagh, and Deirdre killed herself from grief. Fergus, furious at the betrayal of his honour, raised an army which destroyed Emain Macha; and Conchubar was cursed so that none of his line should succeed after him. And so it happened.

Notes: Carrick Uisneach (Cairge vic Uisnich) * the rock of the sons of Usnach.

There were different kinds of oaths in Ireland long ago, but if a person were bound by "gelsa" it was almost impossible to break them. Fergus had sworn always to accept hospitality, and Conchubar knew this.

DEIRDRE

If as you walk by the banks of the Dun
    A shadow falls across the sun
And a cool wind comes like a soft sigh —
Deirdre of the Sorrows is passing by.

H. Browne

Over the Head is an old fort called the Doonfort, and nearby, a chambered cairn. The little loughs here are a delight. One notes especially the Lough na Crannog with its ancient lake dwelling in the middle. The others are Lough Dhu (the Dark Lough) and Lough Fad (the Long Lough). Here, too, the scraping of moving glaciers of old can be seen on the rock faces.

A cottage named "Marconi's Cottage" where it was thought wireless experiments were carried out is at the end of the shore near the Head. In fact, the experiments were carried out in a house in the town. Here one can also see the old coal seams, and the salt-pans where salt was once produced.

I suppose dulse, an edible seaweed, and yellow man, a hard yellow toffee, could now be said to be the chief exports—not to mention lots of good fish!

Fair Head.

The "Wathers o' Moyle" (North Channel) and the mouth of the Margy have long been associated with the legend of the Children of Lir. . . .

THE CHILDREN OF LIR

Lir was a chieftain of the Tuatha de Danaan, a people who lived in Ireland long ago. His wife whom he dearly loved died after sickness of three nights.

Soon after, his friend Bob Dearg, King of the Tuatha de Danaan, feeling sorry for Lir, asked him to come and choose a new wife from his three foster daughters. He chose Aobh and she bore him two children but later died giving birth to twin sons. The children were Fionnuala Aodh, Fiachra and Conn.

Lir was overwhelmed with grief but again his friend had a solution: he offered Lir's wife's sister, Aoife, for a wife. Lir agreed, so she came to Lir's home and at first all went well. She did honour to her sister's children. But gradually she became jealous, and was determined to be rid of them.

She put them in a chariot and drove away to a quiet spot, where she told her attendants to put them to death. They refused. She had not the courage to kill them herself, so she took them to Lough Dairbhreach (Lake of the Oaks) and there turned them into four swans, white and beautiful.

Fionnuala said, "Witch, you have struck us down but we will get help."

The other children said they would be avenged, but asked that some limit be put on their enchantment.

Their stepmother agreed and this was the spell: they were to remain swans until the Woman from the South and the Man from the North came together after they had spent 300 years on Lough Dairbhreach, 300 years on Sruth na Maoile between Ireland and Alban (the northern part of the Irish Sea) and 300 years at Irrus Domnann and Inis Gluaire. But she relented a little, and said they could keep their own speech, and they would sing the sweetest music in the world.

Lir missed his children, and went in search of them. He came to Lough Dairbhreach where they were. Fionnuala told him what had happened and Lir was brokenhearted. So the swans lived out their enchantment and people came from far and near to hear their sweet music.

Sruth na Maoile was a fearsome, wild sea for the swans. They were often swept apart by great storms, but always they met by agreement on Carraig na Ron, the Rock of the Seals, so they managed to keep together.

After 300 years they went to Inis Gluaire. Christianity had, by this time, come to that island, and St. Mochaomhog, who lived there, came one day to the lake of the birds, and saw the swans.

"Are you the children of Lir?" he asked. "I am come to this island for your sakes. Come with me."

The King of Connacht was Lairgnen, and Deoch was his wife. This was the coming together of the Man from the North and the Woman from the South. The Queen had heard of the swans and wanted them to entertain her, so her husband went to get them from the Holy Saint, but he refused to give them up. Then Lairgnen seized them from the altar, two in each hand, but no sooner had he touched them than they changed into three withered old men and one withered old woman.

Lairgnen ran away in terror, but Fionnuala spoke, "Come and baptise us now for we are near death." And so it happened and they were buried, Fionnuala in the middle, Conn on her right, Fiacra on her left and Aodh between her arms. A stone was set over them and their names written in Ogham.

Their 900 years of wandering were over at last.

BALLYCASTLE

Mairge-Town was an old name for **Ballycastle.** From Shane O'Neill's time, about 1565, the town was referred to as **Baile Caislein** or the town of **Sorley Boy.**

After James I had ensured by patent that the Mac-Donnells were the lords of the entire North of Antrim, grants of land were made by Sir Randal MacDonnell to one Hugh McNeill on 9th November, 1612. Sir Randal and his wife, however, reserved the right to come and live in Ballycastle, if they wished. They built a castle on the site of the former castle, which had given the town its name. The eastern gable of this castle remained until 1848 when it was removed, as it was considered to be dangerous.

In 1734 Ballycastle had 62 householders, 16 Catholics, 32 Anglicans, and 14 Presbyterians.

In time a Miss Rose McNeill, a descendant of Hugh McNeill, married Hugh Boyd, the rector of Ramoan. Their son Hugh Boyd in 1734 obtained a lease of the collieries, and, in 1736, obtained a Deed of the village of Ballycastle. He was a great benefactor of the town, and soon made it a prosperous place with many new industries—salt and soap manufacturing, ironworks, weaving, tanning, a glass works and a brewery.

Just recently the ruins of the old glass-making factory were uncovered near the mouth of the River Margy. Specimens of old, dark-green beer bottles were found. The industry was established in 1755 and mainly produced bottles. However, there are some panes of old glass in the windows of Holy Trinity Church in the Diamond thought by some to be Ballycastle glass.

The original little harbour of Ballycastle was at Port Brittas. This was reconstructed by Mr. Boyd, and when he died in 1765 the town had 20 vessels employed in trade.

Rathlin

Sometimes it seems just a stone's throw to the long green island of **Rathlin** across Ballycastle Bay. But Rathlin is a "separate" place with a long and interesting history of its own. The island was once well populated, but, sadly, the numbers have dwindled and "Rachray" is not what it was.

THE RACHRAY MAN

Och, what was it got me at all that time
　To promise I'd marry a Rachray man?
An' now he'll not listen to reason or rhyme,
　He's strivin' to hurry me all that he can,
"Come on, an' ye be to come on!" says he,
"Ye're bound for the Island, to live wi' me.

See Rachray Island beyont in the bay,
　An' the dear knows what they be doin' out there
But fishin' and fightin' an' tearin' away,
　An who's to hindher, an' what do they care?
The goodness can tell what 'ud happen to me
　When Rachray would have me, anee, anee!

I might have took Peter from over the hill,
　A dacant poacher, the kind poor boy;
Could I keep the old places about me still
　I'd never set foot out o' sweet Ballyvoy,
My sorra on Rachray, the could sea caves,
　An' blackneck divers, an' weary ould waves!

I'll never win back now, what ever may fall,
　So give me good luck, for ye'll see me no more;
Sure an Island man is the mischief an' all —
　An' me that was never married before!
Oh think o' my fate when ye dance at a fair,
　In Rachray there's no Christianity there.

　　　　Moira O'Neill.

We think of Bruce and the spider when we think of Rathlin. There is a cave on the island known as Bruce's Cave, but there are also the ruins of an old castle. It was actually in the stable of this castle that Robert Bruce took refuge, discouraged by his defeat in battle. Here the policy of "never giving up" was demonstrated by the spider. He took it as an omen, faced his enemies again and this time overcame them.

Rathlin is a bird paradise much frequented by bird-watchers. Some Rathlin birds are:

Manx Shearwaters, Fulmar Petrels, buzzards, peregrines and many other rare species, including choughs.

The great headlands play their part in the stories and legends of Rathlin. There were once two princesses from Isla who got into trouble while staying on Rathlin. They tried to escape back to their own land but, too late, they were changed into the two great rocks, Mharrie and Katrina Elagh.

Sea Stacks, Bull Point, Rathlin.

PART II

THE PEOPLE OF
THE GLENS

The Glens or Glynns (woods) lie within that larger district known as **Dalriada.** They consist of the **Barony of Glenarm** and part of **Carey** and extend from **Larne** to **Ballycastle.** Dalriada, according to an old Irish poem, extends from the Bush to the Glen Finneachta, the modern village of **Glynn.**

It is probable that the very early inhabitants of this area were the Irish Picts or "Cruthneans" who were akin to the Picts of Scotland.

Dalriada is named from Cairbre Righfada (pronounced Ri-ada, the long-armed) whose father, Conaire II, King of Ireland, was killed in A.D. 220. "Dal" means "descendants" so Dalriada is the land of the descendants of Riada.

In St. Patrick's time the 12 sons of Erc who was fourth in descent from Cairbre were in charge of Irish Dal-Riada. (A few colonies had already been established in Scotland).

Fergus, the youngest of these, received the saint with kindness and thus earned his special blessing. He led an expedition to Scotland with his brothers Loarn and Aongus about 500 A.D. and firmly established the Scottish Kingdom of Dalriada.

Kenneth McAlpin, eleventh in descent from Fergus, conquered the whole Kingdom of Picts in 842 and became king of the whole of Scotland. From this line the House of Stuart and present British Royal Family are descended.

Clan Colla—The Ui Tuirtre
and Fir-Li

The descendants of Fergus and his family continued to rule Dalriada though somewhat weakened by advancing their Scottish Kingdom. They were overcome in time by the two tribes of the Clan Colla, the Ui Tuirtre and Fir Li. When surnames were assumed around the 10th century we do not know what ones were taken by the descendants of the old rulers of the Cairbre Riada.

O'Flinn and O'Linn or Lyn and O'Donnellan were dominant names of Ui Tuirtre. McAlevy and Dunleavy are from a commander of the Ulidians who helped the Fir Li and Ui Tuirtre against the O'Cathans (O'Kanes) from Tyrone but were defeated by the latter.

After the English invasion the Earls of Ulster owned Dalriada. When King John came to Carrickfergus to put down the supposed rebellion of De Lacy, he gave Dal-riada to Alan, Earl of Galloway, who died in 1234. (The lands must then have reverted to the Earls of Ulster).

When Patrick, son of Thomas of Galloway, was murdered at Haddington (1242) and John Bisset and Walter, his uncle, were accused they fled to Ireland where they obtained the Glynns and Rathlin from the Earl of Ulster, de Burgo. From this John the Bissets were known as MacEoin, in Irish 'son of John''. McKeown is the other version of this name. A condition had been laid on the two that they would join the Crusades to the Holy Land and never return. But instead of proceeding to Jerusalem they chose to start life anew in the Holy Land of Ireland!

The MacQuillans are thought to have come originally from Wales and rose to be supreme chiefs in Dalriada. Some believe MacQuillan to be from the Welsh MacLhlewllin. They may have first settled in Connaught where there are mentions of MacQuillans in the old Annals. Later the MacQuillans were over-thrown by the MacDonnells.

The O'Kanes, a Kinnel-Owen family, were opponents of the MacQuillans. There were several branches of the O'Kanes, known as Clan Manus. It is known that some assumed the name McHenry. In 1542 the O'Kanes aided by the McSweeneys defeated the combined MacQuillan and MacDonnell army, at that time helping the MacQuillans. The Battle of Aura (1583) finally established the Mac-Donnells as the chiefs of the Glens.

McAula (McAwley, McAuley) were a Scottish family from Ardincople, Dumbartonshire, to whom lands were given around Larne by Sir James of Knockinsay. The O'Donnellys were another Kinnel-Owen tribe who aided the O'Kanes. The O'Haras were brought by the de Burgos from Connaught and settled around Loughguile. McSporran or McSparran were a Scottish Highland tribe. McCambridge is McAmbrose. McKillop is another Glens name. They were numerous in Glenballyeamon.

Later, the MacDonnells either feuded with the O'Neills or made peace with them. **Sorley Boy** was one of their most

I

famous chieftains who caused Queen Elizabeth many a headache. At one time the Queen sent Sorley some letters which confirmed his rights to certain lands—the Glynns area that had belonged to the Bissets. He had wanted the whole tract from Larne to Bushmills after helping the Queen against the O'Neills. Tradition says that Sorley put the letters on the point of his sword and said that it was by the sword he would hold his lands, not by the Queen's writ.

The Battle of Aura (Orra)

At the top of Glendun can be seen the great spread of Orra mountain. Here was fought that great battle in July, 1583, with the MacQuillans and O'Neills against the MacDonnells.

The MacDonnells covered the Moinnavan Bog which lies between Tievebulliagh and Trostan with rushes to give the appearance of firm ground. Thus many of their enemy rushed in and perished. Local people tell of finding pikes and muskets here for years afterwards.

The battle raged right down the valley of Glenshesk. Victory at last came to the MacDonnells and days of celebration were later spent on top of Trostan on which was raised a memorial cairn, Caslan Sorley Boy, after the MacDonnell leader.

On Orra are two graves said to be those of Hugh Phelim O'Neill and a servant of Hugh O'Neill. "Phelimy Roe's Cairn" is in the townland of Altaveedan about half-a-mile south-east of the road from Armoy to Clough. It is said some letters which he scraped on the stone as he lay dying can still be seen. As a result of this battle estates and castles belonging to the MacQuillans of the Route passed to the MacDonnells.

Since this battle a saying arose in the Glens that "a rush-bush was never known to deceive anyone but a MacQuillan".

After his defeat at Orra, MacQuillan retired from the Route and is said to have lived in a cell at the Abbey of Layde where he died at an advanced age. (Our poet in the Battle of Aura thought otherwise).

THE BATTLE OF AURA

Say, heard you the tidings now Donagha Mor,
  Or saw you the signal shine forth from the shore
Of our kinsmen a thousand hath landed at Torr,
  And the standard is raised on the heights of Torcor.

MacQuillan, the fierce, on the donagh hath sworn,
  Unavenged his fair sister no longer shall mourn;
With lance and with sabre made havoc and flame
  To blot from his scutcheon fair Evelyn's shame.

MacDonnell, the haughty, to Aura hath come,
  With hawberk, battleaxe, standard and drum,
With message insulting the treacherous knave
  Hath dare to combat MacQuillan, the brave.

MacQuillan hath summoned his clans to the fray,
  His best and his bravest from mountain and brae;
From Inishowen's headlands to level Armoy.
  Dunseverick's proud Castle and steep Ballintoy.

They come from the hillsides, they come from the shore
  They come from the rill side of distant Altmore
From valley and corrie, from mountain and height,
  They come in their fury, they come in their might.

They come as the torrent leaps down from the rock,
  They come as the eagle sweeps down on the flock,
They come as the billows dash furious and free
  When the wrath of the tempest is spent on the sea.

There are tall battle spears from the Foyle and the Bann,
  And smart mountaineers from the vale of Glenann,
And sons from far Donegal, the land of the cloud,
  To ride in the train of MacQuillan the proud.

Oh! what a cloud of them passed from the shore,
  MacQuillan is proud of them Donagha Mor,
MacKillop, MacQuillan, O'Neill and O'Hara,
  Haste with their clans to the battle of Aura.

Heard ye the battle shock as it burst forth on the heath,
  Spear thrust and sabre stroke, ruin and death;
Unshriven, neglected, the stricken ones lie;
  Unaided, dejected the beaten ones fly.

Oh! it was a holocaust, Donagha Mor,
　Mad with battle lust, drunken with gore.
They smite and they slay, they rend and they cleave,
　Mercy they ask not, nor mercy receive.

In the halls of Dunluce there's mirth and rejoicing,
　Her Lord at the tilt-ring the lance lightly poising;
In the halls of Dunluce ere the dawn of to-morrow,
　Shall ring the loud caoine and wailings of sorrow.

For the bravest shall lie in the dawnlight together,
　Beneath the blue sky in the depths of the heather,
Unburied and stark in the red fields of slaughter,
　Their life-blood encrimsoning dun sullen water.

Maidens make moan for them, fond fathers mourn them,
　Shout ullagone for them ye who have borne them,
Raise wirra strue slain by the fountain,
　Shout ullalu for them dead on the mountain.

He fought the red fight, but he fought it in vain,
　MacDonnell has conquered, MacQuillan is slain;
Transfixed by a shaft from the hosts of MacCaura
He perished that day on the red field of Aura.

　　　　　　Dusty Rhodes.

THE MACDONNELLS

Nearer our own time the family name most closely associated with the Glens is that of MacDonnell.

Colla MacDonnell was an older brother of **Sorley Boy.** He was the third son of **Alexander MacIan Cathanac Mac-Donnell,** Lord of Islay, Kintyre and the Glens and great great grandson of John, Lord of the Isles, who by his marriage in 1399 with Marjorie, heiress of the McKeowns (Bissets) obtained the Lordship of the Glens or eastern part of County Antrim from **Larne** to the **River Bush.**

Alexander MacIan Cathanac came to the Glens about 1500 and is supposed to have built Dunaneenie Castle at Ballycastle. Alexander had six sons—James, Angus, Colla, Alexander, Sorley and Donnell Gorme.

Sir James of Kintyre succeeded his father and took over his Scottish estates. Colla, he appointed Lord of the Glens under him. Colla erected Kinbane Castle (Ballycastle) between 1545 and 1547. He married Eveleen, a daughter of

MacQuillan, Lord of the Route. (The Route, a modernised form of Dalriada, is usually considered to comprise part of the Barony of Carey and the Baronies of Dunluce, Kilconway and Liberties of Coleraine.)

Colla later laid claim to the MacQuillan lands of the Route. This led to wars, and disputes continued even after Colla's death and finally Sorley Boy defeated the MacQuillans at the great Battle of Aura. Colla himself was probably buried in **Bun-a-Margy Friary** but many of his descendants are buried in Layde Old Churchyard. Direct descendants of Colla through the male line are still to be found in the Glens.

In 1620, Randal, son of Sorley Boy, was created first Earl of Antrim. Today, the descendant of Sorley and Randal is the present Earl of Antrim, though descended through the female line since the 18th century.

The coat of Arms of the MacDonnells can be seen in Craigagh Church and, of course, on several tombstones in **Layde, Bun-a-Margy** and elsewhere.

The **MacAllisters,** a sub-clan of the MacDonnells, were brought from Scotland as support, and many settled in the Route area.

The **MacDonnells of Antrim** are a leading branch of the Scottish Clan-Donnell and, as such, they rank among the most distinguished representatives at the present of the Ancient Clann-Colla.

Domhnaill is the original form of the name. This is pronounced exactly "Donnell".

Lia Fail, the Stone of Fate. It is said to have been brought to Ireland by the Tuatha de Danaan. This stone according to legend was then taken by the Irish to Scotland where eventually Kenneth McAlpine placed it at Scone. On it is written —

**"Should Fate not fail, wher'er this stone is found
The Scots shall monarchs of that realm be found".**

The stone now rests under the coronation chair at Westminster Abbey.

Most Scottish clans had their own war-cry with which after a period of silence they launched themselves into the attack. The MacDonnell cry was **"Fraoch Eilan!"** (Healthy Island). The Clan badge of the MacDonnells and the MacAlisters was the **Fraoch Gorm** (the common heath).

One can trace the Lords of the Isles back to Fergus, who with his colonists founded the Scottish Kingdom of **Dalriada, and was himself descended from the Irish King Conaire.**

THE WAY OF LIFE

The ways of life changed little in the area for about a hundred years.

The Plantations of the 17th century did not seem to affect the Glens greatly, though Elizabeth had wished to give **"Burney Dall"** (Cushendall) to Henry Knowles, Vice-Chamberlain and Treasurer of her Household. Some think that from the prevalence of Scottish names from the 16th century some dispossession took place. The names **"McAuley"** and **"McAlister"** became numerous.

It seemed that clan rivalries and fights which marked the 16th century had by the 17th century largely died out and the area was peaceful.

From old records we can get quite a good picture of life in the Glens in the 18th and 19th centuries. The Reverend Stewart Dobbs, writing about the parish of Layde in 1806, describes the inhabitants and their way of life. At this time there were 119 Protestant families and 511 Roman Catholic families in the parish. The chief food was oatmeal, potatoes, milk, fish and a little wheat.

The houses were simple cabins built of stone with thatched roofs. The fires were situated on the floors at the gable end of the house. They had two rooms lighted by two small windows. The people on the whole were extremely healthy, except that consumption was prevalent.

Irish was the language of the people. Ploughs, harrows and spades were the chief instruments for farming. In stoney ground a spade called a "kib" was used.

Slide cars or slipes, a kind of wheelless sledge for transport on the steep mountain slopes, were used. The Antrim variety differed from that in other parts of the country as it wore "shoes", wooden protections which covered the ends of the shafts trailing on the ground. These were replacable when worn out.

The four-wheeled box-car or "wheel-car" was very popular until recently. Every farm had one of these simple vehicles which served for all farm purposes and for social visits to friends, fairs and church.

"The inhabitants of Layd are considered a shrewd, cunning people, with a great deal of native hospitality.

If manufactures could be established, as they are in-clined to make money, it would assist them in paying rent and give employment to most families; they have very little inclination for going abroad and, consequently, so many remain at home that numbers of them are left in involuntary idleness for nearly half the year".

At this time many men went to sea for a number of years and then returned home. It is said some men used to knit stockings as a winter occupation.

"Kelp is burned along the shore by making oblong pits of stone in which the sea wreck is hacked when dry; it melts like lead and forms a hard cake. Some of it goes to Coleraine, some to Larne; some is shipped to Liverpool.

Potatoes used to be planted on seaweed near the coast. A portion of the mountain or so many sums' grazing was given to each family denomination of the low-land; a sum consists of either 8 weathers; 6 ewes and 6 lambs; or a cow; a horse is one sum and a half.

The salmon spawn in the rivers and the fry leave them in April, scarcely two ounces in weight. They return in the month of June always from the south, in shoals, weighing from 4 to 8 pounds each. They are different from the Bann salmon in being longer in proportion and not so well shaped.

The Acre river is noted for good trout. Most other rivers have a good supply of these."

Other fish caught off shore were lythe, turbot, mullet, mackerel, glashan and herring. Lobsters and crabs were plentiful. The heath-covered mountains provided game, partridge, woodcock and snipe. Potatoes, oats, barley, flax were grown. The area seemed to suit small black cattle raised for beef.

There used to be a stocky breed of pony called the Cushendall pony, mostly grey in colour, having a broad back and shortish legs. They have completely died out.

Kelp-burning was at one time important for providing fertilizer.

"Booleying" was the name given to the custom of sen-ding the young people up into the mountains for the whole summer to graze the cattle on the high pastures. They went up about May and returned about October, when there would be great celebrations at Hallowe'en for the reunion. While up on the hills, they built little huts for shelter. Sods and stones were used and they were thatched with heather. Butter was made from milk, and it was stored in wooden casks which were then buried in the bog to preserve the contents. Old casks are sometimes found by people working in the bog.

Ballyvooley is a townland that refers to the booleying custom as do **Galboly** near Garron and **Tievebulliagh,** the mountain of booleying.

In **Cushendall** there were eight annual fairs held: on 14th February; 17th March; 14th May; 29th June; 14th August; 29th September; 14th November, and 23rd December. There was no weekly market. The town and surrounding districts were well supplied with corn and flax mills. **Cushendall** was also a post town.

Note from **Life in the Glens of Antrim in the 1830s:**

"A car with the Mail from Glenarm arrives in Cushendall at 4 p.m. and leaves Cushendall every morning for Glenarm at 9 a.m. On the arrival of the mail car from Glenarm a car starts with the mail for Ballycastle and returns to Cushendall in the morning in time for the Glenarm car. The fare to Glenarm is 1s and that by the Ballycastle car 1/6".

At one time, too, a steamer used to call at **Cushendall** on its way from **Larne** to **Glasgow.** Small vessels used also to ply between **Cushendall** and **Belfast.**

But **Ballymena** was the "big" town to which the Glensfolk always went on special shopping sprees.

A RUM PAIR

Sure I journey every fortnight to the town of Ballymena,
To bring us home the yellow meal and other things we
      need.
For it takes a lot o' feeding stuff and fal-de-lals and
      groceries
Whenever you've a family and a wheen o' beasts to feed.

And just a week on Saturday, as I was headin' home again,
A warm and early April sun was pourin' from the sky,
The leaf was on the elm and the blossom on the blackthorn,
And the yellow yorls were warblin' and maybe so was I.

For I had sold a heifer and had got a right good price for
      her.
The dealers tried to bate me down, but sowl I made them
      pay;
And now I had the bacon, and the syrup, and the brandy-
      balls,
The biscuits and the treacle, and the sugar, and the tay.

H. Browne.

On the way back from Ballymena, near Cargan, there is an area of trees and shrubbery bordering the road and known as Ben's Plantin'. It was on this lonely part that highwaymen used to wait for the farmers returning home from Ballymena after selling their wares, in order to relieve them of their purses!

THE COAST ROAD, THE GLENDUN VIADUCT AND NARROW GAUGE LINE

There was a kind of coast road from earliest times. Richard Dobbs wrote this of travel in 1633:

"by Glenarm, to which are several high ways, but none good, for the lower ways are deep clay, and the upper ways great and steep hills. From Glenarm he that would coast it, to Colrain, goes from Glenarm over the mountain to Red Bay and must have a guide, or if he keep the sea near his right hand; it is very deep in winter, and yet some steep passages ill to ride up or down; both ways are not to be commended either in summer or in winter. From Red Bay is a very good way to Cushendun, but from thence over the mountains to Carey, you must have a guide to Ballycastle, and well you escape — so the mountains seem a continual bog, where a man is in danger of sinking with his horse, and the Lower way so steep that your horse climbs very oft."

There were other small roads into the Glens but the making of the **Coast Road**, as we know it today, must have been a tremendous feat. When it was built in the 1830s it was known as the **Grand Military Road.**

In the late 1830s came another great feat—the building of the **Glendun Viaduct**. Its tall graceful arches span the glen and the brown Dun river. I know it as a great place for throwing fireworks to make a spectacular display. I have a great affection for the "Big Bridge."

The next major innovation was the **"Narrow Gauge" Railway**, opened in the 1870s mainly to transport minerals being hopefully mined at the time. One line went to **Red Bay** via **Glenariff;** and the other was from **Ballymena** to

Parkmore, a bare isolated place on the top of the mountain. This proved a blessing for one reluctant passenger because in winter it was often snowed up. The passenger, my father—home to his beloved Glens for Christmas—had an excuse to extend his holiday away from his work in Belfast.

Today Parkmore is an eerie deserted village. The narrow gauge no longer functions but once it was the wonder of the times.

THE NARROW GAUGE LINE

Looking up through the trees,
  Leaning out from the door,
I shall never again
  See the train from Parkmore
With its small shining engine
  So sturdy and grand
And it winding its way
  Through the length of the land.

Oh, there once was a time,
  And a time there was then,
When the train, like the river,
  Was part of the Glen,
And the thread that connected us,
  Silver and fine,
With the rest of the world
  Was the narrow-gauge line.

You never knew what
  That small train might be bringing
To the halt by the bushes
  With all the birds singing;
With its soft trail of smoke
  And its rumble of thunder;
And who would get out
  Would be half a day's wonder.

There's no child will ever
  Go running again
To stand on the bridge
  And see the small train
Leap straight at the darkness
  And thunder beneath
And out and away
  To the wind and the heath.

There's no child will wait now
To feel the bridge shake
And shout for adventure's
Sweet perilous sake,
Where silver rails shone
There is wilderness now,
And the whins, the wild ash
And the weed grasses grow.

When I was a child
I'd have said that for ever
The train would endure
Just the same as the river.
But the world's in a hurry
With your life and mine
And it hasn't much use for
A narrow-gauge line.

Siobhain Ni Luain

CASTLEGREEN (CAISEAL(NA)GREINE)

Where the main Ballycastle Road begins its long upward climb over the moor is my "Granny's" in the Glen. In this long sturdy whitewashed farmhouse, standing full in the sun on its bed of gravel, I learnt to know the Glens and their people. It was well named **Caiseal(na)greine** (rock of the sun), now Castlegreen, for in the old days I believe the time could be told from the sun's rays on the old rock in the garden, now covered in turn by daffodils and roses.

Here was the shop, here petrol was sold and wool bought; here you came for coal, tobacco, scythes and flour, ladies stays and men's boots or even a paper. Here was a kaleidoscope of life in the Glens 40 years ago just before modern life began to invade. Dogs could take their ease in the sun in the middle of the road and sparks flew from the boots of the men with the scythes as they marched down the road to cut the hay in the "home".

In spring I saw the lambs arrive. If the weather were bad the men of the Glens had to tramp the mountains for long hours to rescue their animals from deep snowdrifts, their faithful collie dogs their only helpers.

Primroses began to dapple the glens. When summer came there was the hay to be saved. What work there was in those difficult fields where no tractors could go—the scything, the lapping, the tossing, the rucking. Younger men stripped to the waist in the hot sun but the older ones kept well covered—the less chance for the clegs! Perhaps an old straw hat would replace the paddy one for summer.

Foxgloves, bucky roses, fuchsia and honeysuckle grew in profusion in the hedges and fields. We searched for "fruochs" (blaeberries) at the Head Ditch.

Then the turf, too, which had been cut and footed in the early summer, had to be brought home or stacked on the mountain. This meant whole days away, making tea on a turf fire, drawing sweet water from the hidden place among the rocks, being covered in "coomb"—fine turf dust—until you could hardly see and carrying turf in great slatted baskets until the arms ached. And all the time we hoped to find something exciting in the bog—a cask of butter preserved from long ago or the antlers of an Irish elk would have satisfied us well.

Autumn brought the harvest and thanksgiving and the covering of the Glens with berries, glorious rowans, rich red haws and juicy blackberries. The hills were purple with heather.

Winter and the Glens people enjoyed some leisure. There were dances and ceildhes, the old set dances mixing happily with the more modern. The men took out their guns and in the red sunsets brought home their game, rabbits, snipe, grouse and woodcock and the odd pheasant. The women knitted or made quilts with their friends, gossiping over the bright patches. There was good crack round the turf fire on a winter's night, while the wind howled and the crickets chirped.

There would be stories of deals, of fairs and animals, of fairy thorns and some grand concert. Somebody would sing a song, say a verse, put a riddle, tell a joke. A draw on the oul' pipe was grand. Aye!

The holly blazed on the bare hills and we brought a wee bush in for our Christmas tree.

Dancing

Dancing has always been a very popular entertainment in the Glens. Farm kitchens were the first dance halls. In the evening a space would be cleared and the family and their friends danced and sang. The men's boots made sparks fly on the flagged floor as they danced the four-hand reel or the lancers, usually to the music of the fiddle.

In my own family dancing played a very important part for almost 50 years. In the 1920s my father and his brothers built the family dance hall at Castlegreen and until the present troubles it was a place of fun and gaiety for people from all parts of Ulster. In the beginning the family provided the music, the sisters playing the piano and one brother the violin. Then the postman joined them—he was great on the accordion. Finally, the hall became the venue for top show bands, the dancing through time having given way to all that was modern and seventies-style, just as the original oil-lamps had been replaced by the latest in psychedelic lighting.

As a young child I often fell asleep to the melodic thumping of the drums long before the final uninhibited set of lancers had the floor straining and the satisfied dancers dispersed into the cool starlit night.

HAYMAKING IN THE LOW MEADOW

The rain held off. They came to turn the laps
to let the light wind dry them. Every year,
when all the fields, save this, are safely stacked,
the weather breaks and the lapped hay will lie
in its dark bundles day by dismal day,
won only piecemeal by quick spurts of work
because the mounting tide of crowding duty—
pulling, dubbing, spreading the wet lint,
or cutting the ripe corn, or drawing turf
from the high moss home, fills every day
that's free of rain or only gapped with showers.
Now, before corn's ready and the lint
can wait a day or two, they take this chance.
It is a Sunday. It is afternoon.
No loss of virtue's risked. Earth's needs are prime,
and older than the Mass they heard this morning.
Then on the tossed laps they spread out at ease,
cup the small flame to light the half-burnt fag,
or loll and talk and watch the changing sky
as the grey cloud flows slowly down the Glen.
We join them now and slip into the talk
as cautious bathers first dip toe and foot
before they dare the stranger element.
Then the tall farmer with his leaping dogs,
heard just above the road, busy with sheep,
strides over, stoops to handle the coiled hay,
and, straightening, declares for instant action.
We rise and take his orders, lift the laps,
and drop them shaken in a circled heap,
they fork them up to him as slow he rises,

tramping and turning on the growing rick.
His brother then hives off with two or three
to start his own rick half a field away.
I stab and twist and hoist and carry high
and toss my burden in its wanted place,
and stab again, until occasion comes
to turn the twister for the long grass rope
which binds the rocking stack. The other man
with defter help, has beaten us and now
already has a new foundation spread.
There's little talk today. Not silence though,
for who can work with others and hold his tongue?
But not the slow full laden conversation
that, on a dry day, gives to every wisp
of hay or oats the word which must be said,
the prickly proverbs plucked from hedge and bush.
This was the fourth year we had laboured here
in the same fields. I knew what to expect,
for there's but little change from field to field,
and hardly any change from year to year,
but I was wrong. The rain was far too close
to let the patient ritual continue;
already on my forearms and my brows
the small beads gathered, finding each a hair,
When the fourth rick was bound it was the end,
and on the laps we passed to reach the gate
the bright rain glistened. They would have to wait

John Hewitt.

Looking towards Torr Head.

THE CUSHENDALL FARMHOUSE

I was lucky enough to know one of the sons who had lived with his family in this old farmhouse, which has since been moved from Cushkib, overlooking Red Bay, to its new site at the Folk Museum at Cultra. Robert Hyndman and I had many talks about the life and times of his family.

His father had once a famous greyhound called Donal which hadn't thrived too well at the start and had to be kept in the parents' big bed. Yet it lived to become one of the most famous dogs in the Glens. The words of the song by James Delargy can be fitted to the tune of Master McGra.

DAN HYNDMAN'S GREYHOUND

Dan Hyndman's greyhound was born in Cushkib.
It was deep in the heart, it was short on the rib.
It was brand on the back, and the jaws they were brown,
And a short, stumpy tail had Dan Hyndman's greyhound.

Now this dog of Hyndman's had a fine pedigree.
Its father was owned by man named Magee.
Its mother was sported around Tivera
You could trace its ancestors to Master McGra.

Now the boys of the town, they were all on for sport.
There was Stevenson, McKillop, McDermot and Mort.
With their dogs on the slips they set out of the town
And the best dog among them was Hyndman's greyhound.

They hunted on Nappin right up to Magore
  On Greenhan and Aisha and up to Parkmore.
On the green slopes of Trostan there was many's the kill
  On Buchak, on Aisha and the Fair Eagle Hill.

Now the keepers of Aura, brave Willie and Hugh,
  When they heard of their poachers set out to pursue.
When the boys saw them coming they started to run
  And they gave them the slip on the slopes of Glendun.

The keepers assembled a meeting to call
  There were the two Courtneys, Ray and McFall.
McClintock was coming but held by a fog
  Who gave Hyndman the word to watch his good dog.

Now the meeting proceeded, brave Hugh took the chair.
  If we don't act quickly they won't leave us a hare
I've got a "bill" handy wrapped in a sheep's rib
  So now we'll draw cuts for who'll leave it in Cushkib.

Ray he drew first, and his cut it was long.
  Hugh he drew next and his cut it was strong,
Willie drew next and his cut it was small
  But the smallest of all sure it fell to McFall.

McFall was got ready and put in disguise
  He was booted and coated from toes to the eyes.
He put on his sleeved waistcoat that was made in
              Broughshane,
  It was lined with sheepskin to keep out the rain.

A chart was got ready, a line it was drew.
  He was to pass by Tievebula and down by Maroo.
He was to starboard a point, when reaching the town,
  Hoping it would finish Dan Hyndman's greyhound.

When he reached Cushkib they all seemed in bed
  The lights they were out, and the cattle were fed.
Placing his parcel close to the wall
  When a voice at his ear says, "How are you, McFall?"

'What brings you tonight so far from your bog?
  Did your boss send you here to destroy my good dog?"
He called his two sons who were hardy and strong
  And they with two sticks sent McFall fast along.

Now Dan kept his good dog till its youth it was past.
  And he sold it to a friend who lived in Belfast.
Who treated him kindly till he went under the ground
  But the keepers remember Dan Hyndman's greyhound.

STORIES FROM THE HYNDMAN HEARTH

The people of the Glens were and still are great storytellers. Many a good yarn has been spun about the Hyndman's hearth. There wasn't a lot of food and drink given to strangers, contrary to what one might think, as times were hard and people found it difficult enough to keep their own families. There wasn't even much poteen-making going on at that time. (It was more widespread later.) Still, a good few of the carts that rattled past the Hyndman's gate had some of the essential ingredients hidden under a battle or two of straw. Ingredients were simple—bran, treacle, yeast and brown sugar.

The stories at the ceildhes were good all right but at times could be so scary that the neighbours would be nearly too frightened to start for home. Tivera, the fairy hill, was too damned close for comfort anyhow. Then just across the road was that queer well that a beast would hardly have passed except you beat it. Fairies there were certainly—certainly, as many an eyewitness would have sworn. There was one young fellow **Johnny Flanagan,** Donald McIlheran's nephew, who was away minding cows up Glenariff. Well, the fairies got him and it was six weeks before he was back and he never grew at all after that. There was a wee girl, too, up Glenaan way, just 13 when the fairies took her. She was away a wheen of weeks and when she came back she was lame.

Robert Hyndman himself saw the fairies once. He had been away at his girl friend's house up Glenaan and was coming back after his porridge late one Easter Sunday night when he saw the whole place lit up by fairy lights— all over Tivera, all up Glenaan, everywhere you looked. He was a happy man to reach home safely that night.

They were a superstitious lot in the Glens in the old days. If you had looked into their byre you would have seen the red yarn on the cow's horn and on the goat's too. That was to keep off the blink. There's a story about an old boyo, "Oul Ranal" who could put the blink on anything. There was this old mare he couldn't stand the sight of. One day he and the man that owned the mare and the mare were all going down the road. All of a sudden the mare lay down. Stone dead she was. The man that owned her rounded on Ranal.

"Ah! hell to your soul for an oul bugger, Ranal, you've blinked me mare." The owner was real mad and threatened Ranal so much he had to take off the blink then

K

and there. Soon up got the mare, lively as ever, gave the harness a good shake and away they went.

Katie McGreer was another good one at the charms. She was great at taking off the blink. **Dan,** the father, had an old sow lying in the kitchen. She'd just pigged but would have eaten the pigs if they'd gone near her and there were the wee things starving to death for not a drop would she give them. Dan's wife begged him to go to Katie for a charm. Reluctantly enough he went. He wasn't half-way on his road home before the sow rolled over, started grunting and let down her milk to the wee ones and that was an end of the trouble.

There was this other time Robert was away on the mountain shooting and he tripped in a hole and twisted his ankle. It swelled away up—like a bap. He managed down as far as the wee pub for a drink and a bit of a rest, but the ankle swelled up that much that it broke the very boot-laces. For days after it was very painful and looked no better, so he was helped on to a horse and sent over to Katie for a charm. She said the words, tied a red yarn round the bad ankle and by the time he was back home Robert was able to jump down off that horse as right as rain with neither pain, ache nor swelling in his foot.

"Skeoghs" (fairy thorns) were respected. Very few would deliberately interfere with them. One fell in **Henry Dan's** field and he thought it a bit of easy got fuel for his fire so he chopped it up and took it home. The wife put a couple of logs on and the next minute she swore that blood ran out of them and she would use no more.

There was another neighbour, **Patrick McVicker,** who cut down a skeogh in his field and his wife became paralysed and didn't speak for the next 30 years.

An interesting tale is told about **Margaret Hyndman,** the mother. One day one of the boys was coming in through the garden gate and he stood to one side to let his mother pass in front of him. She preceded him into the house. He followed right behind. When he got through the door there was his mother at the kitchen table up to her elbows in flour, baking. He got a right shock. "Mother, how did you get in here baking when you're just after coming in with me from the garden?" "Oh," she explained, "you must have seen my daylight wraith. But that's lucky. It means I will live long. If you had seen it at night, that's different. It would mean I would die soon." It turned out that Margaret Hyndman (Murdoch to her maiden name) lived to the ripe old age of 97.

Hallowe'en was a great time at Cushkib. It was known as the **"Cushkib Fair."** On Halloweve' night young and old from all arts and parts used to gather to play games and dance. Many's the young couple were paired off here and many's a black eye given and received in the process. All the usual games like ducking for apples and trying to catch apples swinging free from a string were played but the old rituals which foretold the future were the most indulged in.

If a boy wanted to know whether anything was going to come of his friendship with a girl he would place a long nut on a warm part of the hearth. She would put down a round one close but not touching. When they were brown and toasted a lighted match was applied to each. If the flame swirled round from the boy's nut to the girl's that was supposed to be him getting an arm around her. (There would be "oohs" and "aahs" from everybody watching). If the nuts eventually moved round to touch, the couple would marry.

Another popular game was "Coorama, coorama, who's got the button?" a guessing game. If the boy in the middle of a circle guessed right he could claim a kiss from the girl of his choice. (Curamach—careful)

But it was a time, too, for playing tricks and jokes on your neighbours like removing their doors and gates and blaming it on the fairies.

"Cushkib Fair" was a gay night for the Hyndman family for their house was the centre of all the fun. **Dan,** the father, was a jokey boy. He had a favourite game played with five spoons. Four were hidden anywhere in the house but the fifth was placed in the hearth so it got nice and black and **hot.** "And now where's the fifth one?" said Dan when the four were found. Then the victim would spot it sticking innocently out of the hearth and make a grab of triumph. At this Dan would double up with laughter and the poor fellow would be yelping round the kitchen with the pain of the burn.

The family had another game peculiar to themselves. it was called "Tilda's game" and went something like this. Tilda and a partner were blindfolded. Each was given a plate. Both were supposed to have soot on the plate and they were to see what kind of a mess they could make of their partner. But only Tilda's had real soot. The partner's might have flour. As a result she usually made a right looking darkie of her friend.

Easter Monday was another great gathering day for a bit of fun, specially among the young folk. It was said that

that was the day you rolled your eggs down Tivera and rolled the girls as well, if you got the chance. The eggs were dyed with whin blossom.

It is good to know there are still long-legged Hyndmans in the Glens even if the old ways are passing from sight and memory.

CUSHKIB FAIR

One gable towards the road, one towards the slope
that meets the shoulder of the storied hill,
door facing east, well out of the winds' way
which funnel steady from the great bare glens
sparse trees about it and a sprawl of walls,
a quarry-pit and a burn across the road,
this house was once a noisy family
of tall sons famous for their endless sport,
horse-play with harness, ballads, dances, games,
glad to be living, even if they knew
the acres were too few to hold them long.

John Hewitt

STONEYBATTER

High up on the hillside above my grandfather's home was a little group of houses called **Stoneybatter**. They were already in ruins and deserted when I first saw them, but these were a typical "clachan" of olden times where a group of mountain farmers had lived until the beginning of this century.

They must have been very poor and led very simple lives. You can see the stone pig sty, the wee shed that did for a cow or a goat, the flat stone where the chickens were fed, and the sad lonely houses now open to the sky. There are the keeping boles at either side of the big hearth-opening where precious bits and pieces were kept like pins and thread and cord.

A unique feature of these old houses is the method by which they used to tie on their thatch. Old cattle bones had been driven into spaces between stones to make firm pegs and the thatch was attached to these.

Lying outside is the old braidh for grinding corn. This braidh was a round flat stone with a hole in the middle. A handle could be inserted and the grain placed below on another flat stone and ground by a turning process.

The people here must have used the soft Gaelic speech and had a very simple life that is also gone for ever. It is sad to see the fuchsias growing up the old chimneys and the wee sweet gooseberries growing wild in the neglected garden. The garden and the potato patch must have been shared in this lofty "commune". I am told that two Miss McDonnells were the last inhabitants.

THE CHARACTER OF THE GLENSMAN

A Glensman is, above all, an individualist. The reason for this is probably the hard way of live on those lonely hillside farms. Men had to be strong-minded and self-reliant as well as physically strong. "Characters" or "eccentrics" were affectionately tolerated for the light relief their antics brought the community.

There was one old fellow who came to my grandfather's shop once a week with a big sack for his groceries. He lived alone far up the Glen. A rather long thumb nail was an awesome feature of the right hand. When asked why he kept it so long he answered "Sure I keep it for peelin' praties, Aye!"

On another Glen farm lived two old brothers and a sister. Every night they had a ritual. The old sister had to bake a "scone", a soda farl, to eat fresh before they went to bed.

The neighbours recorded it in this rhyme.

"Put on the pan", says Robert.
"It's time enough", says John
"Put on the pan", says Robert
"Till Sally bakes a scone."

Another old boy with the reputation of being mean would greet his visitors with "Sure I'd make you tay but och! sure, you're tired o' tay!"

Many houses I visited had the big open turf fire and the crane or crook by which was suspended the big black pot or kettle. One old lady I knew boiled her potatoes in a giant three-legged pot. Near the fire she kept a cow's horn which she fixed over one leg and thus acted as a pot-holder when she was draining the potatoes. The handle was in her other hand. Many households drained the potatoes into the "street", the slanted drainage area just outside the door.

Sam Henry, the folklorist, mentioned some odd names for "dishes" in the Ballycastle area—meelacreesty or crack-in-the-pan and he-fadge. The latter is what is known as potato-oaten in other areas.

Sowans was the traditional supper for **Candlemas Eve,** and also at **Hallowe'en** (Samhain) It consisted of oatmeal, buttermilk and berries.

One of the first songs I remember describes a typical mountain farmer—perhaps:

"I've an elegant field of potatoes
  I've a champion field of oats.
A little bit of clover grass
  To help to feed the goats.
I've a still for making whiskey
  That nobody can find out.
If somebody would only fancy Murphy.

I've got sheep upon the mountain.
  I've got cows upon the grass.
A field for growing praties
  And a billy goat and an ass.
I've that still for making whiskey
  That nobody can find out.
If some girl could only fancy Murphy!

"A Glensman Speaks"

(from "The Black North" by De Blacam)

"The people of the plain country inland and down in Leinster are very decent folk but when they want help with the harvest or any other hard work done they send for the sturdy breed that comes from the hills.

The people that hills breed are strong and able, but you must go to the mountain sides for a finer type again. The cottages up there give you big-bodied men of intellect— workers and thinkers. High up in the mountain, from the quiet hardy places, you get the giants who must be either priests or soldiers. The higher you go the more splendid is the manhood, the fairer are the quiet-eyed maidens. A Highland breed is the world's best . . . "

"Excuse me," said a little man with a big pipe, "excuse

me for interrupting of your striking theory, but may I ask where you come from, yourself?"

"The home where I was reared," said the big speaker, "was the little white topmost cottage at the very head of the glen."

"I thought as much," said the wee man, and went on smoking.

The Scenery

"You have wonderful scenery here," said a towns-woman who stepped from a glittering saloon car to view the distant depths of the valley through an eye-glass on a handle.

"If you had to plough and dig the scenery, ma'am," said the glensman, "you would be content with less of it."

ANDY MAGUIRE

Andy Maguire
Sits by the fire,
Where he'd once ha' been out
In the stable or byre;
"For I'm oul' now," says he,
"And I'm easy to tire."

"I'm oul' now," says he,
"And in need o' a rest,
But it isn't so long
Since I'd hair on my chest
And could handle the ploughin'
Along with the best."

"At ploughin' or reapin'
Or cuttin' the grass,
Sure I never was known
To be out o' my class —
Aye, or dancin' the Lancers
Or coortin' a lass."

"And now I am oul,'
Would you heed what I say:
If it's workin' or coortin'
Then do it th' day,
Ere the chance — or the notion —
Goes slippin' away."

H. Browne

For The Ones Who Went Away

My heart goes out to the little homes
   that star the mountains high,
Where the cloud swirls down when the sun goes in,
   and the blue smoke greets the sky.
With their snug brown thatch, and the low half door
   where the wide-eyed children play,
And the welcome light in the window waits
   for the Ones who went away.

The sea lies calm when the dawn light
   comes creeping down the hill;
When the larks rise high in the pearly sky
   and the morning air is chill.
Then the Mother kneels and stirs to flame
   the smould'ring peats o' grey
That light her eyes as she breathes a prayer
   for the Ones who went away.

Oh dear to me are the dark hills,
   as dear the dewy glen
When the blackthorn tree is a joy to see
   and the whins are gold again;
But my heart goes out to the little homes
   below the rocks o' grey
Where still the light in the window waits
   for the Ones who went away.

                 Sydney Bell

EMIGRATION

Many people had to leave the Glens during the awful Potato Famine. I am told by an old lady, now in her 95th year, of the custom of "convoying," that is, a crowd of friends and relations accompanying to the boat someone who was emigrating. A lot went from Larne in the old days, usually to America—"the States", as Ulster folk say. Many relatives and friends went as far as Larne, from where the boat sailed, and the party usually stayed at McNeill's Hotel the night before sailing. Dancing and singing went on until about 2 o'clock in the morning, and then only the very close relatives of the one that was leaving were left in the room with him. Then the lamenting began. It could be the last time they would be together on this earth. It was a very sad time—almost like a death.

SOME WORDS AND EXPRESSIONS USED
IN THE GLENS

My grandmother always interspersed her conversation—and she could go on for hours and hours—with
Gaelic words.

"Fred, A chree", was always her way of addressing my
father.

"Ochanee, ochanee", was a way of expressing
resignation or lament. **"Astore"** was used occasionally.

As there has always been a close link and constant
comings and goings between Scotland and this part of
Ireland the Irish Gaelic and the Scots have been somewhat
fused. Odd words are used for everyday things such as
"fruochs" for "blaeberries"; **"calligaleen"** for "earwig";
"braw"—"brave" meaning "good" as for day or health;
"wheen"—a few, some.

To **"go for a sail"** could be to go for a ride, for example,
in a cart.

"slap"— a gap in a hedge.

"claigs"— horseflies.

"cowp"— turn over.

"cailleach—the last sheaf left standing in a
field at which sickles were
thrown in a game. (literally "Old
Woman")

"skeogh"— a fairy thorn.

"flioch"— still describes a wet day.

to **"mind"**— to remember.

"ah dammit to hell!"—expletive.

"sheugh"— a muddy ditch.

"boor-tree"— elderberry.

"pad"— a path.

"stooning"— throbbing.

"loanin'"— a lane.

"quare"— very, as in "quare and smart".

"hirplin"— limping.

"thole"— tolerate (Scandinavian).

"hoke"— to dig, principally with hands or
a stick.

"crack"— talk, conversation.

"starved"— frozen with cold.

"hag"— to break roughly as "to hag
sticks".

"girn"— to whinge or cry.

L

"ken" — to know.

"wean" — a child.

"stour" — dust.

"I'll houl you" — I'll bet you.

"dander" — a leisurely walk or "temper".

"throughother" — utterly disorganised or slovenly.

"awful throng" — very crowded.

"boys o' boys" — exclamation of wonder or delight.

a "scrape" — a short letter.

"Holy smoke!" — expletive.

"Do you tell me that?" — surprise, wonderment.

"Isn't it well for her?" — Hasn't she good luck?

"march ditch" — boundary.

"quet" — to stop.

"garding" — garden.

"stack-garden" — where the stack was built for the winter.

"houl yer whist" — Keep quiet!

"yellow-yorling" — yellowhammer.

"to langle" — to hobble with cord as for sheep or goats.

"a tangle" — a tall, gangly person.

"the street" — a cobbled area outside the back-door, usually sloped, for drainage.

"sorra on it" — a curse.

"art" — direction, as for weather.

"father" — to provide fodder for the animals.

"haup" — (hop) to wrap up or tuck in garments.

"ceildhe" — a social gathering.

"boy" — yellow as in Sorley Boy, yellow Charlie.

"dhu" — black.

"gorm" — blue,

"roe" — reddish.

"dun" — either a fort or brown as in Dun river.

"knock" — a hill.

"park" — a pasture field as in Parkmore (mor big).

"tieve" — a hill.

"tor" — a pointed hill or headland.

>"**bally**" — a town, or small group of houses, a townland.
>"**kil**" — a church.
>"**craig**" — a rock.

Some of these are, of course, in use all over Ireland, but having lived in the Glens I know that they are in common use there.

RATHLIN AND TAISIE

Rathlin, although an island, has for many years been considered part of the Glens, ownership being usually granted together.

Rathlin has a long history of its own, some of the best remembered parts being the saddest. In legend Rathlin, or **Raghary,** owes its origin to the mother of **Finn MacCool,** the "Giant". It is said that Finn had drained Ireland dry of whiskey; so his mother set off for Scotland to try to get some there. She carried in her apron "a mountain — with rivers, trees and all" to use as a stepping stone. Less than half-way across she tripped and fell, dropping her burden which formed an island, and she was pinned underneath it. To this day when a storm blows up it is said, "**The oul' witch is kickin'.**"

Being situated strategically between Scotland and Ireland, invaders often made the island a stopping place. Rathlin had its own ruler, or Chief, and the Danes are said to have caused great slaughter there trying to take the island.

Robert Bruce, as we have been told, fled here when things were going against him and later, his courage restored, achieved success.

In 1551 **Sorley Boy MacDonnell** occupied the island with his Highlanders. The Lord Deputy Sussex, after the capture of Sorley Boy, sent four ships to attack the island, but the English were repulsed, and only the Commander survived. Later he was exchanged for Sorley. Sussex took a terrible vengance on the islanders, and later slaughtered the whole garrison left on Rathlin.

On 22nd July, 1575, there was yet another island tragedy. Sorley Boy had at this time most of his own family and the wives and children of his principal Clansmen, with their family treasures, on Rathlin for safety. This was discovered by the English and a great slaughter took place. It is said that Sorley, distracted, ran up and down the strand at Ballycastle powerless to help and it is estimated that as many as 600 lost their lives in this holocaust.

In 1642 the most terrible massacre of all took place. Charles I had ordered the Earl of Argyll to take a large force to Ireland to subdue rebels there. Rathlin was chosen as the first stop and depot for the troops. But when they arrived and found Charles's enemies there the whole population was put to the sword. It is said that many women were thrown into the sea at the cliffs, named **Slock-na-Calliagh. Crook-na-screedlin** (Hill of Screaming) was where many women watched the battle. As the leader of the invasion was Sir Duncan Campbell it goes without saying that Campbells are not very popular on Rathlin!

The Battle of Glen Taisie

In 1565, Glen Taisie was the scene of a frightful encounter between O'Neill forces, led by Shane O'Neill, and the MacDonnells, led by the three brothers, James, Sorley Boy and Angus. James and his brother Sorley were taken prisoner and Angus was killed. James died of his wounds in a dungeon. Sorley Boy was later freed, but the Macdonnells were revenged at Cushendun two years later when they murdered Shane O'Neill.

There is a monument to another MacDonnell killed at Glen Taisie, **John Roe MacDonnell.** He seems to have got as far as Glenshesk, to the Lag-na-Cappul (hollow of the horses), where there is a standing stone known as John Roe's Monument.

Taisie, Princess of Rathlin

There was once a King of Huaradha, which is believed to be Norway. His name was **Nabghodon** and he was grieving deeply over the death of his wife. Courtiers told him the women of Ireland were very beautiful and he ought to have one for his new wife. So 30 men proceeded to Ireland in their great sailing ships. They first came to Rathlin, where they saw a splendid palace on the island and they decided to stop there.

It was not long until they saw "a lady, the most hand-some of the children of Adam, having clear blue eyes, curling tresses of hair, a melodious voice and a pleasing accent. She and her band of female attendants sat in an enchanting glade, and they commenced to play on their musical instruments, while she employed herself in in-structing her female companions."

This was **Taisie Taobhgheal** (of the white side), daughter of Donn, King of the Island and descendant of Dagdha, King of the Tuatha de Danaan.

The strangers demanded the princess as bride for their king, but were refused; she was already promised to one, **Congal.** Relations were strained but the strangers were given hospitality and the next day set sail for home.

Congal, who was aspiring to leadership of Ireland, was at that time warring with **Fergus MacLaide.** When the King of Rathlin heard of an army being prepared by the King of Norway to take Taisie by force, he at once got in touch with Congal. Several chiefs accompanied Congal and went at once to Rathlin for the marriage of Congal and Taisie and to help defend the island. The Norwegians came as the celebrations were actually taking place, and a fight took place, in which Nabghodon was personally slain by Congal, which led to a complete rout of the invaders.

Congal now thought to ask a piece of land from Fergus MacLaide as a present to his wife, and one supposes as a bargain for the promise of peace between Fergus and himself. Fergus complied and she was given the area now known as **Glen Taisie.** Here her father built her a palace called **Dun Taise.** Today it is thought that the palace built for her was the great fort of **Broomore** under the shadow of Knocklayd.

So this peaceful little island has seen quite a few bloody battles in its long history. It is sad that today not very many live there.

It is rather interesting that the island is divided in two, and the people are referred to by two different names; there are the Lower-end **"cuddins"** and the Upper-end **"foorins".** "Cuddins" were "fish fry" and "foorins" were "seabirds". The latter were supposed to speak the better Gaelic. But here too, although a few Gaelic words are used, the language spoken is now English.

SAINT PATRICK

In "**The Tripartite Life**" of the Saint it is recorded:

"**He journeyed into the Glens westward, where Cenel-muinremur is today. His two nostrils bled on the way; Patrick's flag (Lec Patrick) is there and Patrick's hazel. He put up there. Strath Patrick, it is named to this day; Domnach Patrick was its former name. Patrick remained there on Sunday, and this was his only church in that region.**"

There is a theory among Patrician scholars that the Glens referred to here are the Glens of Antrim, as the Cenel-muinremur mentioned was the tribe of Muinreamhar, eighth in descent from the Cairbre Riada who were rulers in the Murlough area. Near Torr Head is Leckpatrick, Patrick's Flag-stone.

In writing of the modern Catholic Church in Glendun, the parish of Innispollan or Inchpollan, O'Laverty believes it to have an unusual status, and wonders if this could be the church founded by St. Patrick, called Strath Patrick. The townland of "**strath**" or "**Straid**" is nearby. In a field near the Church is a "**Gloonan**" stone, which is supposed to have the impressions of the Saint's knees. Innispollan also borders Culfeightrin, founded by the Saint.

I have also read a theory that the wood of "**Foclut**," known by the Saint in his captivity, may be in this area, as there is a townland with a similar name—**Faughall**.

The Catholic church of Innispollan (Craigagh) is the only Catholic church in the diocese to occupy an ancient site.

A STORY OF KIERAN

It seems that at one time the community at **Layde** was hard pressed by famine. **St. Kieran** went to the Abbot of Ardclinis, explained that it would be another month before their corn was ripe, and asked for their prayers. The holy abbot told Kieran to look across the bay and said, "Your corn is already ripe." Kieran looked and could see the yellow patches of ripened grain and thankfully hastened home.

He and his monks reaped this miraculous crop, and the place to this day reminds us of the miracle. **Moneyvart** (Muine-bhearraid) means the moorland of the reaping.

It is believed that this Kieran is the same as Kieran of Clonmacnoise as their festival day is the same—9th September.

SAINT McKENNA

St. McKenna is associated with the founding of the old church of Ardclinis mentioned earlier. The name of this saint might be **Mo Enna.** This seems to link up with **St. MacNissi** whose other name was Enan.

On the ditch opposite the old church are several whitened stones called Cahir MacKenna (McKenna's chair).

HEATHER BEER

At one time around the 9th century the Danes had become quite powerful in parts of Ulster. But they suffered a great defeat when their leader **Turgesius** and his men were overcome by **Nial, King of Ulster.**

The last survivors of the Danish invaders were said to have been an old man and his son who, fleeing before the victors, took refuge at **Garron Point** on the Antrim coast. These two held a special secret—how to manufacture beer from heather.

At last they were captured and were told that their lives would be spared if they revealed their secret. The father said that he would only reveal it if, first, his son were slain. This was done. Then the old man, too, asked to be put to death, saying that he would take his secret with him to the grave. So the recipe was lost for ever.

FINN MacCOOL

Finn or **Fingal** is not only a hero in Ireland. His exploits are told in Scotland and the Isle of Man. In Western Scotland various places are called after him—**Fingal's Stair** in Argyllshire, the **Wall of the Fianna** in Skye, and at the head of Portree Loch is **Fingal's Seat.**

Finn's father was said to have been the leader of the Fianna and to have been slain by a rival who was head of Clan Morna. Finn's sister hid the child Finn in a safe, wild place away from his father's enemies. In the wild woods where they lived in a tree house he grew up large and strong, skilled in running, swimming and leaping, a veritable "giant"

He gained wisdom, too, from eating from the Salmon of Knowledge, caught for him by an old man fishing in the Boyne. Later, an Ulster smith made for him a wonderful sword which Finn earned after working for the smith for a year and a day.

His name "Finn" was given to him by his enemies who said, "Who is this fair one?" From that day Finn, the fair one, was his name. He later won the leadership of the Fianna and was renowned for his bravery.

Many deeds are attributed to him: the building of the **Giant's Causeway** and the throwing of a piece of land at a rival giant. This latter exploit left Ireland with **Lough Neagh,** and accounts for the **Isle of Man** in the middle of the Irish Sea.

In the parish of Loughguile there is a townland called **Lavan,** which is said to have got its name in this way:

"Finn was dead and before he was buried an old woman took his hand and said, 'The Hand of Finn'. In Irish 'Lamh' (lav) is a hand; so the place is known as Lavan, the hand of Finn."

There used to be a large stone called **Finn MacCool's Stone,** but it was removed some time ago. Three other stones were also at this spot, and it is recorded that in 1813 a certain **Andrew Duncan** removed one of them and found under it a cinerary urn.

Finn loved his two great hounds and the story of Doonfin in Glenshesk tells of his love for **Bran.** The other hound's name was **Skolaun.**

The story of Finn's son, **Ossian,** is told in the chapter on Glenaan. Oscar, Ossian's son, was killed in battle and was greatly mourned by Finn:

> **Best loved of all, O best loved of all,**
> **Son of my son, slender and fair;**
> **My heart runs wild and I despair.**
> **Oscar lies slain to rise no more.**

Only twice did Finn weep. At the death of Oscar and the death of Bran.

FLORA MACDONALD

There is a tradition that **Flora Macdonald** brought **Bonnie Prince Charlie** to her kinsmen in the Glens after fleeing from Scotland and that he spent a night there, possibly at the old ruined house of the farm near Castlegreen, called Mullards.

There may have been a big house at the top of a mysterious avenue behind Mullards; he may have stayed there; but not a trace of this remains. (I have seen this place referred to as Castlegreen).

As part corroboration that this was true I am told that in the old graveyard of Templeastra, Port Bradden, there is a gravestone erected by Flora MacDonald in memory of a servant who died while accompanying her on her journey in the Glens. I wonder could the old Castle have been razed because it had sheltered the Prince. In one secret corner near the mysterious avenue is a well with the sweetest water in the world. But where did that avenue lead?

This area had been owned by a Captain MacDonnell who had fought with James II. When he followed his King into exile his lands were forfeit. Could he have had a large house here and was it destroyed?

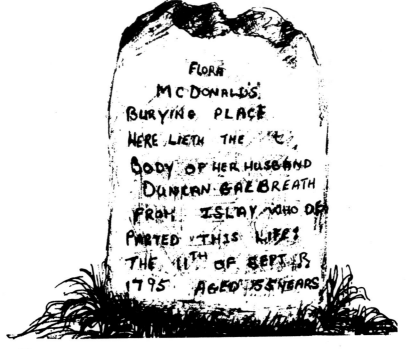

M

This is the gravestone I found in the old churchyard but, as can be seen, it states that it was the burying place of her husband, Now I am inclined to think this was not "The" Flora Macdonald as this was not the name of her husband.

"The" Flora Macdonald is said to have saved the life of Prince Charles Edward on 28th June, 1746. She was arrested after the event and imprisoned until July, 1747, and then released. Later she married a Macdonald and went to America, but returned to Skye where she died. She had seven children and left many descendants.

THE GLENS FEIS

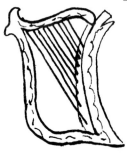

This festival of song, dance, music and language is held annually in July in the little town of **Waterfoot** or **Glenariff**.

It is spread over a few days with two days for the language competitions, one day for the singing and music, and finishing with the sports and dancing on the first Sunday in July.

The Feis began in 1904, sponsored by, among other enthusiasts, Miss Margaret Dobbs of Cushendall and Miss Ada McNeill of Cushendun House. Dr. Douglas Hyde was present at the very first Feis, as was Roger Casement.

A story is told that Roger Casement brought by boat all the inhabitants of **Rathlin** to Waterfoot for the first Feis and, as they got off the boat, he presented each with a half-crown to enjoy the fun. It was certainly a red-letter day for the inhabitants of Rathlin, for their own harper became the champion harper of the Glens that day.

It was hoped that the Feis would go round the Glens and for a time it was held in such centres as **Glenarm, Carnlough** and **Ballycastle.** But it seemed that Waterfoot was the most central place, and so the Feis became established there.

People came from all over Ireland to join in the fun and competitions and most certainly this Feis has been an important factor in keeping the Irish language alive in the Glens.

The Feis in the Glen

When I was young I took a day from Time
And keep it still—No glint of all the sun
That shone that day, but shines in the fixed clime
In which I keep the hours he can't outrun.
Oh, I went down that morning to the Feis
With everyone to watch the way I'd go!
I wore a linen frock with cuffs of lace
I wore a yellow hat with a cherry bow.

　　　The day the sun shone as it never shone, ever,
　　　On sea and on glen and on bright waterfall,
　　　The day I was wise, and the day I was clever,
　　　The day I knew all things, and nothing at all.

Through the green, golden glen the birds were singing
And all the little brooks were tuned to me.
The pipers in their saffron kilts were swinging
Down to the glen's foot where it meets the sea.
And, oh, the prizes! Fat books for my winning,
For I knew everything there was to know—
We are so sure of things at the beginning—
I wore a yellow hat with cherry bow.

　　　Siobhan Ni Luain
who lived in Glenravel (the tenth glen!)

Glenariff from the ridge of Lurigethan.

PART III

BELIEFS AND CUSTOMS

The people of the Glens, of course, share many beliefs in common with the people in the rest of Ulster, but here we shall look at customs associated particularly with the Glens area.

FAIRIES AND FAIRY THORNS

As can be seen from the account of the Hyndman family there was quite a respect for the fairies and things connected with them. Sometimes they were known as "**groga,**" and in Glenshesk were supposed to be responsible for the building of a church. A dialect dictionary tells us:

"**In Antrim and Down the Grogan is a kind of fairy, two feet high and very strong; helps farmers harvesting and threshing but offended if offered any recompense.**"

There was the custon of "smooring" the fire at night. A woman's last duty was to bury a live turf in the ashes so that next morning it could be quickly fanned into a blaze. This was done to avert the wrath of the fairies if there were no fire for them to sit at through the night.

Harry Browne when collecting folklore in the Glens some time ago for the **Ulster Journal of Archaeology,** records this story:

"**In a homely cottage not far from Glenarm a young man told me that although he himself had never seen the Wee Folk he would not like to say they do not exist. He remembered his grandfather telling about having seen them more than once; indeed, on one occasion the old man watched a battle between two opposing sections of them, as they marched and countermarched up and down in the** moonlight for nearly an hour. 'Aye' he went on, 'and you were speaking about Fairy Thorns. Well, all I can tell you is I was talking to a man at Cushendall Fair not six months ago; him and me was having a bit of a drink together after the Fair, and he told me he had cut down a Fairy Bush one time, and the next day when he got up out of bed his face was round at back of his neck. Well, he got cured of it—I'm not going to tell you how he got cured—but to this day if he goes into that same field or anywhere near where the old thorn tree was, he 'tumbles the wild-cats', and falls about all over the place".

There was once a man in Glendun who wanted to clear a field of Fairy Thorns to build a house. But lorries broke down, workmen got injured mysteriously and the house was never built.

A friend of mine now living in Cushendall but who had for years lived in Glendun told me the following stories.

"There was this man who wanted to take down a 'skeogh' or Fairy Thorn that was on his farm in Glendun. He hagged away at it. Well, after a blow or two the blade 'turned' on him. Then he got another axe and blood started coming out of the tree. That finished him. He went away home to his bed. But the next morning all his hair had fallen out, and he had to wear a wig for the rest of his days.

Another man cut a "skeogh" and his hair turned white overnight."

Then my informant's son wanted to build a wee house to keep rabbits in. He chose the site and started to dig, not realising he was near a "skeogh." Suddenly he heard a voice saying, "Don't dig here!" He paid no heed, thinking he was hearing things. But again a voice said, "Don't dig here!" This time he was sure it was a friend of his playing a trick on him and he went to look for him. But not a one was about. When he started again and the voice became louder, "Don't dig here!" he stopped at once and with his spade headed home. He gave up the idea of the hut on that spot!

My Glendun friend told me of his mother and sister hearing "Fairy" music as they would be coming from a ceildhe at a neighbour's house late at night. It was described as the "sweetest music in the world". But, said the old man with a twinkle in his eye, "the fairies have all gone now because the people are so bad . . . ".

Fairies must have lived close to the houses of people, as another story tells of a woman staying with a friend. She had just washed the dishes and went to throw the dish-water out near the door when a wee voice yelled, "Don't throw it here! It'll go down our chimney!"

Professor Estyn Evans describes a "**Fairy Thorn**" as one not planted by man, and which grows on its own or on some ancient cairn or "rath." Occasionally a group is known as "Fairy Thorns" or "gentle" trees. But my father always maintained that a Fairy Thorn was one where the trunk was single for a long way up, not branching or dividing near the ground. Other glensmen have confirmed this. It must be one trunk up to about four feet from the ground. It is thicker, too, than the ordinary thorn, more a tree than a bush.

Harry Browne again writes

"There was once a Fairy Thorn which grew in a hedge by the roadside. It had once stood alone, but a road had been driven through the field, and to make a hedge other bushes had been planted. The local people always respected this tree and it was never pruned with the rest of the hedge, until it finally became a nuisance and orders were given to cut it down; but the old roadman refused to have anything to do with such sacrilege. Finally the old roadman died and a younger man took his place and, with the aid of the man who tells this story, removed the Fairy Thorn. Some branches of the Fairy Thorn were mixed with others and given to a neighbour to put under his haystacks. Two months later the neighbour's daughter died and, added the storyteller, 'Don't you ever breathe a word of this, for if he ever found out what was done he would blame us for his daughter's death and he would put a bullet apiece in us!' "

THE HARE WOMAN

Tales about the **Hare Woman** are common all over Ireland and are told here, too. It was said that an old woman could change herself into a hare and suck cow's milk. Shooting at her was no good. The only answer was to load the gun with silver sixpences. The hare was shot in the leg and that same evening an old woman was carried into the house with a bullet in her leg.

THE CHARM FOR MILK

"There was the old woman who, by murmuring an incantation at the right time, could draw milk from the cows to herself by some secret method. 'I know a man who was going along the road. He was riding his horse and had a big pair of knee boots on. It was bright moonlight at the time, and all of a sudden he saw an old woman standing up on one of the knowes* with her arms stretched out in front of her and saying, 'Come a' to me, come a' to me.' He didn't know the old woman, but he pulled up his horse to get a better view of what was going on. He was no great believer in them sort of cántrips, and being a kind of jokey fellow and thinking he might as well take a hand in the proceedings, he threw up his arms and started to say, 'Come some to me, come some to me.' With that his knee boots were filled with milk. He put spurs to his horse and never stopped till he was in his own house."

Dobbs tells of a man who saw fairies dancing under a Fairy Thorn and knew he was in for bad luck. He suffered the following winter for his house was hit during a terrible thunderstorm and his family badly frightened. Of course, this storm hit far and wide but he thought it was meant specially for him.

It is of interest to note that there were neolithic men, called **Firbolgs**, who were supposed to have hidden in holes or other underground dwellings when conquerors came to Ireland. From this the folk memory of curious wee men could have originated. **Fearsihe**, pronounced "Faery", means the men of the hillock.

The foxglove, which grows all over the Glens, is sometimes called the "Fairy Thimble." Other names are "Fairy Glove" or "Folk's Glove."

The hawthorn is the "Hag-thorn" and its berries are regarded as being associated with sacrificial drops of blood. The ash-leaf and the rowanberry are protective aids.

The whin, which grows in profusion on the hillsides, has been referred to in my presence as "the curse of Ireland," but I don't think it has "fairy" associations. In Famine days their petals provided food for men and horses. At Easter the children used the gold blossom for dyeing eggs.

Note: *Knowe, a small hillock or hump.

CHARMS

Diseases which have been cured by charms include erysipelas, warts, bleeding, sprains and jaundice. The charmers charged nothing, but if they once used their powers to cure a human being they couldn't cure an animal and vice versa.

Methods varied. Warts were caused to vanish by their number being told or by applying the juice of some herb. Others rubbed warts with half a potato which had to be wrapped up in a parcel and thrown away. Woe betide the finder of this parcel, as the warts would be transferred to him!

Warts are very curious things. They can appear and disappear overnight.

"Erysipelas" or the "Rose," as the disease is known, is said to be cured by charms.

Jaundice was said to have been cured by mixing the urine of the patient with soda or wheaten bread which was then secretly fed to him! A case of what you don't know . . . !

Sprains, of course, are helped by the tying on of coloured thread. I referred to this in the Hyndman notes.

A charm for bleeding is known and practised by certain people.

THE BLINK

There was also among the glensfolk a superstition about cow's milk being "blinked" so that it would not produce butter for several days' churning, unless some old woman charmed the blink away.

I remember my grandmother did not like certain people to come into the house when she was churning as they put the "blink" on the butter.

Another charm relates to cows being "elf-shot". The inhabitants are able to show you a spot where the cow had been struck; at this point there is a hole in the flesh but the skin is unbroken. The cow gives no milk until relieved by the charm.

O'Laverty gives a rather interesting cure.

"Sick cattle are supposed to have been shot by fairies with the stone arrow-heads which are frequently found in the fields. The cure is a drink of hot water and oaten meal given to the cow out of a vessel in which is placed a number

of stone arrow-heads—perhaps the hot drink would cure without the arrow-heads but many people in County Antrim do not think so".

If a person with the power to "blink" admired a new litter of animals it was always safest to give him one. When a cow calved a little hay or straw was burned round her to keep off fairies. Another cure for "blinking" was to give the cow three mouthfuls of salt and water and to throw what was left in the bucket on to the hearth.

An old ordnance survey of 1835 states:

There is a legend that a chapel will not stand in Ardclinis. Strange to say, there is one in Red Bay just finished, the walls of which fell twice in the building, and the vessel which brought the slates and other materials was totally wrecked, and all lost.

There is a tradition that a hermit once cursed the river in Ardclinis parish; and the belief is strengthened by there not being a trout in some of the rivers in this parish. It is also believed that a cock will not crow in Ardclinis parish.

There is some reference to the Glens area in "Ulster Folklore" by Jeanne Cooper Foster.

People had once a fear of their souls being captured and this led to an unwillingness to have a likeness taken, in other words, a photograph. A story is told of an Glenswoman who would not be photographed, but who was later persuaded to hold a three-legged pot for it to be photographed! This fear is very common today among primitive races.

A Ballycastle woman, describing a Banshee she had seen, said that she was a little, wizened, red-haired woman, who ran before her into a bog, wailing and wringing her hands.

Around Ballycastle they call a similar type of fairy a "grogach". It helps with the outside tasks of the farm, and is described as being large and uncouth, with a hairy skin. It, too, disappears when rewarded for its work.

N

Some odd cures are mentioned by **Sam Henry,** the folklorist. Around Ballyvoy it was said that **"a person whose mother's maiden name was the same as her husband's is the proper party to point a gooseberry jag at a stye in the eye to effect a cure".**

Rathlin people go even further and say **"a magical charm can only be worked by a woman whose parents were of the same name, who marries a man of her own name, and on having her first baby flaps her apron three times on the object which is to be magically charmed".**

It was also said that a rope of hair wound round a churn would bring back the butter to the milk of "blinked" cows.

HOLY WELL

"Near Cushendall is a small well called Toberdoney, or Sunday Well, which has its origin from being visited on that day for the cure of complaints, chiefly of children. A little pebble is thrown into the well and a pin stuck in a bit of cloth beside it. Thousands of these shreds may be seen there; but the practice is in part given over and the well is now assisting the race to turn a corn mill." (from a 19th century description)

Another tradition is that all places with the name, Donagh (Sunday) were founded by St. Patrick and that the foundation was on a Sunday.

———————

Some local customs are here described by a contemporary.

Glenarm, Antrim Coast

And fairy thorns in field or fen
Are passed in silent fright;
While darkling in that yawning glen
There gleams a quivering light
Where roofless ruined Majey's Mill
Lurks 'mid the lowering flood.
And nightly ghosts and witches chill
The lonely traveller's blood.

And youths on Easter morn will rise
To see the dancing sun,
And gaze until their dazzled eyes
Believe the dance begun;
And some at Easter or May Eve
Through meadows green will roam,
Cull buttercups and daisies weave,
Or bring first catkins home;

Or dye their eggs with bloom of whin,
And throw them high and watch;
Play "round the ring", "tig out" or "in,"
And kiss the girls they catch;
And nuts at Hallow Eve they'll burn,
See apple-duckers dipped.
Or bite at crossing sticks that turn
With fire and apples tipped.

But blackberries none dare to eat
When Hallow Eve is past,
For then the Devil (says ancient freet)
Has worms upon them cast.
And Christmas rhymers then will play
Saint George or Robin Hood,
And shoot or "shinny" all the day,
Or light the logs of wood.

W. Clarke Robinson.

This gives a delightful picture of seasonal games and superstitions. The Christmas Rhymers may have been known around Glenarm but it is a custom not known in the Glens farther north.

SAINT BRIGID'S CROSS

The **St. Brigid's Crosses** vary in shape, the most common being the four-legged or three-legged type. They are woven of rushes and are fashioned on St. Brigid's Eve, the last day of January. Originally a pagan symbol, the Cross has now taken on a Christian overtone. They are hung over the doorways of houses or in the byres to protect the homes from fire and the inhabitants and their cattle from evil spirits. (Brigid was a cowherd and had therefore a personal interest in cattle).

In an old account written of a Naturalists' Field Club outing we read of an old lady in a cottage in Glenaan showing her St. Bride's Cross, made of rushes. She called it "the calliagh" but this term was, I thought, reserved for the "cailleach", the last sheaf in the harvest field. By calling this the "calliagh" it is said to show Aryan ancestry!

The crosses were plaited left over right. I discovered that in the Glens it was once customary to make a small bed of rushes and place it near the fire on St. Brigid's Eve so that the Saint could come in and rest.

Dobbs says:

"The people are not all as strict in keeping the Holy Days as formerly; in general their observance is a nuisance, as the day is spent in the public house and little is done the next day. When two or three Holy Days happen in a week, it is a fine opening for a week's idleness".

MAY EVE AND MAY DAY

The **May Festival,** the Gaelic Beltane, was a time of many magic beliefs and superstitions. If you put a snail under a bowl on May Eve the next morning you could read the initials of your future marriage partner.

Mayflowers used to be crushed to provide a juice with which the cow's udders were washed. Other places used the juice of buttercups as a protection or to ensure a good milk supply. May dew was considered a great beautifier by the ladies!

Sprigs of rowan, which had protective properties, were stuck in the midden or over the byre to save the farm from mischievous fairies. Mayflowers were gathered on 1st May and scattered on doors and windows. A translation of a poem from the Irish reads—

"For this was Beltain Eve and brakes and bowers,
Copses and dells were ransacked of their flowers
To deck tomorrow's Feast each gate and door
With garlands and green leaves were covered o'er".

THE CAILLEACH OR CALLIAGH

The last sheaf of corn is called the **"cailleach"** (old woman), in the Glens. In other parts of Ireland it is the "churn" or "hag".

Various games and ceremonies were connected with this. The sheaf was left standing uncut, then plaited in three strands. There followed a competition to see who could cut it by throwing sickles at it. This game had some early connection with the worship of the "corn spirit." Indeed, when the word "hare" is used instead of "cailleach" we should recognise our word for "harvest" which is, in fact, "Hare Feast".

The idea of the Corn Spirit was so real to children in the Glens that they stood around waiting to see "it" run away to the farmer whose corn was not yet cut. In Scotland a strip of corn was always left uncut on each farm so that no farmer would have the ill-luck to be "last" to cut the corn!

The "cailleach" was then hung in the farm kitchen and it is said no beast would go hungry on that farm.

Fairs

Cushendall held fairs eight times in a year. Girls going to the fair used to carry their white stockings and good shoes in their hands until near the place. They washed in the nearest stream, then dressed ready for the big day! On the Coleraine road the girls washed at a well called "the Spout" on their way to the Lammas Fair. There is now no trace of that well.

"The May rents are paid in August by the produce of butter; the November rents are paid in February by the sale of pork."

THE LAMMAS FAIR

The **Lammas Fair** today is associated with Ballycastle. But long ago this feast of "Lu" was on 1st August throughout Ireland. Now it is held on Lammas Sunday, the last in July. This is also known as Garland Sunday or Bilberry Sunday.

This time marked the end of summer and beginning of harvest. Offerings of flowers and fruit were made at Holy Wells. Often, too, the people gathered on some high place for games and fun. Blaeberries, called fruochs in the Glens, were gathered.

This Lammas Fair at Ballycastle is now held on the last Tuesday in August, extended recently to the Monday also. It could be that the late harvest in the area influenced the date.

The Fair could first have had its origin here in the need to bring supplies from Scotland to support the MacDonnell troops fighting in the Glens and Route. For many years afterwards the men of Islay were regular visitors to the Fair and there are records of them coming until the late 19th century.

Another event could have influenced the holding of a regular Fair for trade and fun. Sorley Boy ordered a great festival to be held at Ballycastle to celebrate the coming of age of his nephew, Gillespie Feacle, the MacDonnell heir.

There were days of games and celebrations. But, unfortunately, a bull broke loose and wounded Gillespie who later died of his wounds on Rathlin. However, he had already married and his wife later gave birth to a male heir to carry on the line.

There used to be six annual fairs at Ballycastle, held near the old castle of Dunaneenie, the fort of the Fairs.

The Lammas Fair has an unbroken history of over 300 years. Today it is still a popular event, drawing many tourists to the town. A brisk trade is done in selling livestock, horses, sheep and cattle. Alongside this are the stalls of the traders set out in the Diamond. "Yellowman," a sort of hard yellow toffee, the secret recipes of which are closely guarded, is one of the Fair's specialities. "Hard Nuts" were little biscuits also associated with this Fair. But today as well as the traditional fare are all the modern varieties of confectionery. The stalls all do a brisk trade and there is an open-air carnival atmosphere. In a nearby street horses are trotted up and down to show their paces and many a bargain is struck with the slap of the hand and the return of a "luck-penny".

In rural areas, where people did not travel very far afield, the Fair was a great event and 100 years ago used to last a week with dancing and all sorts of amusements going on. The whole population of Rathlin came over to Ballycastle regularly for the fair and brought cattle to sell. If the weather was bad they did not mind having an extra few days on the mainland.

We must pay tribute to another speciality of the Lammas Fair—"dulse", that edible seaweed, most of which is gathered locally for sale to the fair-goers.

John MacAuley, the bog-oak carver, who gathered and caused to be preserved for us so many old songs, is above all remembered by the very famous "The Ould Lammas Fair"

**"At the Ould Lammas Fair, boys, were you ever there,
At the Ould Lammas Fair in Ballycastle, oh?
Did you treat your Mary Ann to dulse and 'yellow man,'
At the Ould Lammas Fair at Ballycastle, oh?"**

Fair Day, Ballycastle Diamond.

HALLOWEVE

"Halloweve" is always what the true glensman calls "Hallowe'en." It was a night when the living felt the dead very close; so strange things could happen. If at midnight a girl looked over her left shoulder into a mirror she could see the face of her future husband beside her own.

Peel an apple at Halloweve and throw the peel, which must be all in a piece, over the left shoulder. Then it will form the initials of your future marriage partner.

For a girl another superstition was that if she found two teaspoons in her saucer and heard the cuckoo the next day she would be married within the year. (I always thought that two teaspoons in a saucer meant a christening—but maybe there's a link!) Many other games of divination were played. (See the Hyndman account for the games played with nuts.)

The Irish name for this time was **Samhain.** Part of the festivities were, of course, to celebrate the return of those who had been away all summer on the high pasture with the cattle (booleying). Because it is the eve of All Saints, Samhain is also known as Hallowe'en. (All Hallows — All Saints).

All Souls is a different day—2nd November—and it is
wrong to equate All Saint's Eve with All Souls as is so often
done.

A bonfire and dressing up for the children is still a
traditional part of the fun. There is a certain "air" about
on Hallowe'en but the old superstitions are fading away.
Turnip lanterns are still made, What for I wonder. To
scare someone or something away? They do resemble an
empty skull!

THE WAKE

Written on the occasion of the death of Dan Hyndman.

We snicked the latch where one was dead
constrained by ancient courtesy;
the open coffin on the bed
shewed us the man we'd come to see.

We gave our greetings to the gloom;
I found a seat against the wall;
my wife was hustled to "the room"
where women were foregathered all.

Since turf and wick gave feeble light,
the crouching shapes seemed much the same;
with anxious ear and questing sight
I sought to join each shape and name.

Of stock and weather was the talk,
Of harvest fabulously great—
the distances men used to walk—
the dangers of our pampered state.

Then one would rise and say Goodnight,
and one who stood would take his chair;
the smoking turf would flicker bright
with each fresh gust of chilly air.

Then suddenly the only sound
would be of crickets at the grate;
and James would reach and hand around
tobacco on a dinner plate.

John Hewitt

O

BANSHEES AND WAKES

The **Banshee** is the eerie spirit of doom that belongs to Ireland. It is the wailing of this "woman" (the Banshee) that is supposed to foretell death. Long ago in Ireland there was a people called the Sidhe who were renowned and feared for their mystical powers, and it was the women of this tribe with their unearthly wailing that gave their name to the ghost we call the Banshee (bansidhe, or women of the Sidhe).

When death came to a house the corpse would not be touched for an hour. Meanwhile, all mirrors and pictures would be turned to the wall, the clocks stopped and later the bedding of the dead person burnt.

In all parts it was the custom to "wake" the dead or have a "wake". Friends and neighbours gathered at the home of the deceased. Visitors would go first into the room where the corpse lay and place a hand on the brow to symbolise friendship between the living and the dead. Then they would eat and drink and smoke all that was provided for them. Even a supply of clay pipes was available so all could join in. This custom was in many ways a helpful distraction for the relatives of the deceased.

An interesting little story was told to me in Cushendall. There was this wee woman who in death was indeed tiny, like a dainty wee doll. When she was put in the coffin—in those days just a plain wooden box, not padded—she didn't fit it at all and they thought the body might roll around in it when it was being carried. So one man went out and got a wee armful of hay, nice and soft, and put her lying on it. And there she was peeping out of the hay like a wee doll in a box.

Corpses were always taken out feet first and a roundabout way to the churchyard was taken. There was a belief that the spirits of the dead hovered about and might return to the house. So the closing of shutters, the pulling down of blinds, and the roundabout way to the graveyard, combined with the changes in the houses, all were meant to confuse the spirit and dissuade it from returning.

Dobbs gives us this interesting note:

"Whenever a person dies in a townland, no work is done till the body is interred."

"Before a dead body leaves the house all the pins, tyings etc., are removed and loosed to prevent its spirit being restrained or detained in purgatory. A priest is generally buried with his boots on him." (from a 19th century account of customs in the Glens)

WEDDINGS AND CHRISTENINGS

Weddings were often accompanied by a certain amount of horseplay. I am told that at the wedding of my own grandparents not only was rice thrown but also an old shoe which caught the unfortunate bridegroom on the head!

A wedding took place in Glendun and the newly-weds had gone to their new home up the glen. That night the local boys started their tricks. They fired guns and brought the bridegroom out. Then they locked him in a shed. After that they removed all the gates in sight and generally upset the pair. There is a possible connection between gun-firing and the more ancient rite of driving away evil spirits from the new home!

If an expectant mother arrived at a house it was considered unlucky if the hosts did not rise and greet her and give her a share of the meal.

"They will not rock their first child in a new cradle but will send any distance for an old one, and should they not get one they will put the child in a basket. If they have to leave the child alone for even a minute, they will place a pair of tongs across the cradle or basket to prevent the fairies from carrying it away. If a child does not cry when it is being baptised they consider it a very unlucky omen."

(from a 19th century account of customs in the Glens)

THE CAUL

A child born in a "caul" was said to be specially lucky and to be protected from being hung, drawn and quartered, drowned at sea, or burnt alive. Even meeting a person who had been born thus was sure to bring luck.

_____

While, of course, many of the old beliefs have faded away there are still traces to be found even today. After all, who knows? And sure I'm glad I nearly lifted the roof of the wee church at Cushendall at my christening!

The Glens have a character that is unique. It is not just Nature's riot of wild beauty that captures the heart. It is that blend of sensible, neighbourly, country living where people have time for "depth" that draws us from the strivings of twentieth century life to look for peace.

Changes are coming to the Glens and if "improvements" and "amenities" tame and hedge then soon the Glens will be just like everywhere else and that wonderful heritage will be lost for ever.

THE GLENSMAN

There is nine glens in Antrim — aye, an' more!
There is lochs in them and rivers by the score;
But the wan that bates them all
Lies just back o' Cushendall,
An' thon is where my thoughts are evermore.

Och, Glendun is very sweet — an' so's Glenaan!
Glenshesk would cure the hurt of any man.
But Glenariff is the queen —
That is plainly to be seen —
Find a better and ye're welcome — if you can!

There' a music in my heart. far away;
There' a stoonin' in my heart, night an' day;
'Tis the waters where they fall
In the glens round Cushendall,
An' the cryin' o' the gulls across the bay.

Ach, it's hard to sail away an' lave it so
But them that heeds the sea is boun' to go;
An' them that knows the glens
May reach their journey's en's,
But they leave behind the peace they used to know.

Sydney Bell

THE AUTHOR

Maureen Donnelly is one of Ulster's most prolific writers on local history. While The Nine Glens is probably her best known work, other books include Downpatrick and Lecale, Saint Patrick and the Downpatrick Area, Inch Abbey and Parish, Patrick, Brigid and Columcille and numerous other pamphlets and articles for the tourist industry including Finn MacCool and Places of Historic Interest Around Newcastle etc.

She has broadcast widely on folklore and history on both local and national networks and is a scriptwriter for B.B.C. Schools.

Her love of Ulster and all its people, combined with comprehensive experience in teaching and lecturing has enabled this writer to produce easily absorbed and enjoyable material for all age groups and backgrounds.